INTERPRETIVE
Theme Writer's
FIELD GUIDE

Jon Kohl

NATIONAL ASSOCIATION FOR
INTERPRETATION

230 Cherry Street
Fort Collins, CO 80521

NAI is a private nonprofit 501(c)(3) organization
and professional association. NAI's mission is
to inspire leadership and excellence to advance
heritage interpretation as a profession.

ISBN: 978-1-879931-33-6

Contents

First Word from Sam Ham 1
Why I Agreed to Support this Field Guide

Preface 3
Where Does this Field Guide Come from?

Acknowledgments 7

Foreword by Shelton Johnson 9
Floating the Tigris: Harnessing the Light of Thematic Interpretation

Note from Clark Hancock 13
Need for Interpretive Theme Writing Support

Trailhead 15
Who Uses This Field Guide and How

Station 1 19
What Is Thematic Interpretation, Anyway? And What Is It Not?

Station 2 27
We Write Themes for Primary and Secondary Audiences

Station 3 35
Strong Interpretive Themes Embody Big Ideas and Vehicles to Deliver Them

Station 4 45
Interpreters Must Ignite Their Inspiration for the Big Idea, Not Just Write It

Station 5 67
The Big Idea Develops within the Audience's Mind via a Vehicle

Station 6 87
Theme Writing Can be Individual-, Team-, or Community-Based

Station 7 95
Interpretive Frameworks Leverage the Power of Community for Interpretation

Conclusion 111
Interpretive Intelligence Can Defend Against Artificial Intelligence

Field Notes 115

Last Word from Ted Cable 159
Theme Writing: A Trail That Never Ends

Why I Agreed to Support this *Field Guide*

When Jon asked permission to write this *Field Guide* that builds so squarely on top of my own work the past four decades, I thought it was an odd request—not just because he didn't actually need my permission, but more because of a twinge of uncertainty about seeing my own words and ideas presented in new contexts and in formats that would differ from how I myself would put them.

Any apprehension I might have had then, however, has long ago been replaced with the satisfaction of seeing where Jon has taken his own thinking about the premise and promise of thematic interpretation. In fact, having a professional interpreter want to build on my work—and hopefully improve it in some way—is not only a bona fide contribution to interpreters and the field, but also a critical passing on of the interpretation field's leadership torch from one of numerous greying professors to the next generation. Talk about sustainable development.

Even though I have no financial interest in this volume, knowing Jon through our conversations over the years about themes and thematic interpretation, and knowing that he offered himself as a vehicle to advance these same topics that have dominated my professional activity all these years, in the end it was a no-brainer decision. I hope you agree.

Sam H. Ham
Professor Emeritus
University of Idaho

Sam Ham's 2013 book Interpretation:
Making a Difference on Purpose

Where Does this *Field Guide* Come from?

When the US Peace Corps assigned me in 1993 to my new Costa Rican office at the aging Simon Bolivar National Zoo and Botanical Garden in order to co-build its education department, my new boss Luisa dropped *Interpretación Ambiental* on my desk and informed me that interpretation was now part of my new job. I hadn't heard of environmental interpretation before or the amusingly named fellow who wrote the book. I quickly came to understand, nonetheless, that rhyme and all, Sam Ham was the only one who could teach me, although remotely, about interpretation in that venerable bar-and-cement zoo in downtown San José.

Years later, many interpretation books grace my office shelf, yet interpreters including myself still find little support to carry out the central act of interpretive theme writing. Sam's 2013 sequel, *Interpretation: Making a Difference on Purpose,* dedicates an entire chapter to crafting strong interpretive themes and offers seven proven guidelines for doing so. But the focus of the book is farther reaching than just theme writing. To date, no single volume in any language has devoted itself entirely to the transformation of its readers into theme writers. In short, that void this *Field Guide* fills.

Little did I know that years earlier I had already been preparing myself to write this pocket field assistant, which in hindsight now seems like an inevitable outcome of my journey. I say this because my writing career germinated in fifth-grade when

I won a town-wide evaluation/contest in fiction writing. Jump to high school, when I founded our literary magazine and edited our school newspaper at the same time. Once I arrived at Dartmouth College, I joined the literary magazine, wrote for the same humor magazine that Dr. Seuss once edited, wrote opinions for the school newspaper, and interned at the *Dartmouth Alumni Magazine, Oceanus* magazine of the Woods Hole Oceanographic Institution, and *Greenpeace Magazine* in Washington, D.C. I even founded *Sense of Place*, the very first formatted e-magazine (*Hypercard*) transmitted over an electronic network in the history of the Internet, a historical feat long since forgotten in the fast-evolving world of smart phones and database hacks.

Over the years, I have written scores of trade, popular, and academic articles, training manuals, and creative writing pieces (including *Fallout*, a near-future sci-fi romance published in 2013) in both English and Spanish. Unbeknownst to anyone but my fortune teller, I had also been training myself for a career in interpretation. After being hired in 1997 by RARE Center for Tropical Conservation to become a nature guide trainer in Central America, I began writing what today would be dozens of articles about interpretation, including a column in NAI's *Legacy* magazine called the "International Interpreter" under then-editor Alan Leftridge. My first article on theme writing came in 2004 in *Legacy* called "Mighty Messages Make Memorable Presentations," which Sam would later cite in his book and use in his workshops. I would continue writing about themes in my blog, "International Heritage Interpretation" (www.faceboook.com/heritageinterpretation).

In addition to writing, I have been an interpretive trainer in numerous countries in the Americas developing a holistic training model aimed at promoting real social development. I have also been an interpretive planner at sites in the US and abroad.

As I deepened my involvement in the interpretation field, it became clear that despite various attempts (for example, National Park Service's Interpretive Development Program), the field has not enjoyed a commonly defined set of basic skills, including theme writing, and at the time of this writing in 2018, the debate about interpretive performance standards rages on. So, the timing of this *Field Guide* may be appropriate and, with any luck, contribute to standards that emerge.

While Sam's books establish the scientific rationale for why thematic communication is necessary and outline a practical foundation for theme writing, the document in your hands is really the first of its kind to dedicate itself whole-heartedly to the art and craft of interpretive theme writing. Likewise, Beverly Serrell writes a full chapter on "Big Ideas" for exhibits, and Alan Leftridge penned a book on interpretive writing, but neither addresses the integral nature of why and how to write the most important sentences an interpreter may ever have to ink on paper. Many other writers touch on the theme of themes, yet their examples suffer weakness by this pocketbook's standards and many of the same "experts" continue to confuse themes and topics (as differentiated in Sam's first book, *Environmental Interpretation*). None provide models of how this *Field Guide* envisions a strong theme to be, based on Sam's two fundamental criteria of provocation power.

The *Field Guide* further makes what I consider a novel addition to interpretation literature by recognizing that themes arise not just from keyboards of individual interpreters, educators, and interpretive planners, but also from teams of these people and even by communities within a larger social process. The PUP Global Heritage Consortium, of which I humbly serve as director, has rescued the 1936 National Park Service concept of a "thematic framework" and evolved it into a participatory, community-based form of heritage self-expression that produces interpretive themes both reflecting heritage values of their heritage "owners" as well as marking the boundaries for any kind of subsequent interpretive planning.

Jon has written two cover stories for NAI's Legacy *magazine. Also, this book on theme writing represents Jon's 35th NAI publication going back to 2001.*

Ultimately the *Interpretive Theme Writer's Field Guide* did not begin spinning wheels until 2015 when the National Association for Interpretation allowed me the space to hold a webinar on Strong Theme Writing. In that moment, I differentiated the concepts of Big Ideas and a vehicle to deliver them that about equates to Sam's Relevance and Ease of Processing as the twin towers of provocation power, the essence of strong theme writing. After that webinar, which enjoyed considerable participation, the idea of the *Field Guide* finally emerged as a viable and desirable evolution of Sam's work as well as of interpretation literature in general.

Of course, I would never have been able to convert idea into publication were it not for several giving people, over which **Sam Ham** stands tall. Only through years of mentoring and debate about themes, did he build enough confidence in me to support this progression of his thematic legacy. He did this despite having graciously offered me a fully funded PhD studentship in 2002 only to suffer my turning down his offer in order to continue working in the field with RARE. Later on, and to my relief, he agreed to become a partner in a guide training program offered by Fermata, Inc., the company that provided me the opportunity to become an interpretive planner and later still when he joined the PUP Global Heritage Consortium as an advisor to promote interpretation internationally. To cap off our relationship, Sam accepted my 2016 book, *The Future Has Other Plans: Planning Holistically to Conserve Natural and Cultural History* (co-authored with Steve McCool), as the ninth installment in his Applied Communication Series published by Fulcrum Publishing in which both of his eminent interpretation books can be likewise found.

In a near second comes my wife and life colleague in interpretation, **Marisol Mayorga**. An accomplished interpreter in her own right, having studied for her doctoral degree in interpretation under Dr. Ted Cable and having been director of the postgraduate interpretation program at the University of Costa Rica for six years, has willingly subjected herself to my incessant chatter about the need for better theme writing and as a sort of taste tester for many of my own themes, including many of those in this *Field Guide*. I would be remiss in not mentioning as well that she first-authored with me Latin America's first and only university textbook on heritage interpretation, *Esencia de la Interpretación del Patrimonio: Una visión holística para experimentar y conservar el patrimonio natural y cultural de América Latina*, written in Spanish for Latin America and published by a prestigious Costa Rican university press (EUNED, 2019), rather than the far more common practice of importing and translating tomes from other countries.

I would also mention my good friend and Colombian country representative for the PUP Global Heritage Consortium, **Carlos Rosero**, who has helped to develop interpretive frameworks especially for local communities; **Matt Villamaino** who re-designed the Interpretive Theme Writer's Worksheet into a version I can proudly share with the public; **Emily Jacobs**, the training coordinator for NAI, who allotted the moment to offer that 2015 webinar; and my writing mentors, **Jay Heinrichs** who served both as my editor at the *Dartmouth Alumni Magazine* and long-time friend and advisor over the years, as well as **Casey Yager**, who was my fiction writing critique group mentor and co-author of my abovementioned sci-fi romance novel. Both have honed my writing reflected in this *Field Guide*.

I must raise a high-five to **Shelton Johnson**, a most accomplished creative writer and US National Park Service interpretive ranger whose own work has inspired many interpreters across the United States. I am honored and indebted to his writing the foreword here.

I would further thank the PUP Global Heritage Consortium which both provided materials (such as the worksheet), example themes, theme training methods, and a number of its members who contributed to this book, such as Sam Ham (advisor), **Clark Hancock** (PUP treasurer, moderator of the Interpretive Theme Writing Think Tank, and author of the note page 13 as well as reviewer), Marisol Mayorga (technical support member), **Ted Cable** (general member and author of the "Last Word" in this book), and Carlos mentioned above.

I offer my sincerest of thanks to **Paul Caputo**, deputy director of NAI, *Legacy* editor, and its communications guru. Aside from editing this book, Paul has published the majority of my several dozen articles in *Legacy*, *Journal of Interpretation Research*, *The Interpreter*, and *Interpretive Sourcebook*.

Finally, all photos are by me unless otherwise noted. Special thanks to Wikimedia Commons.

To produce a mighty book, you must choose a mighty theme. No great and enduring volume can ever be written on the flea, though many there be that have tried it.
—Herman Melville

Floating the Tigris: Harnessing the Light of Thematic Interpretation

Interpretation is an art, which combines many arts, whether the materials presented are scientific, historical, or architectural. Any art is in some degree teachable...
— Freeman Tilden's Third Principle

This statement by Freeman Tilden has always resonated with me because of my background in the arts, primarily English literature and classical music. Those creative paths have given structure and vitality to all of my interpretive programs. From them I've learned that all art must have structure, or *form*, like a glass, and then the slow, measured apprehension of the *content*, like wine, which is fragrance, taste, color, temperature, but mostly *flow*.

NATIONAL PARK SERVICE

The joy of a good wine stems from the movement of that *stuff* from one sense to another, as your palette deconstructs a story of passage from grape to bottle to *you* swallowing, absorbing, becoming a biography of soil, sunlight, atmosphere, and earthly life distilled to a liquid that when drunk sparks from receptor to receptor like lightning.

The theme of *any* work of art, including an interpretive program, is that vital essence capturing everything, reflecting everything. The theme's the spirit of a novel, a dance, a symphony; as well as the residue of what's been boiled down, refined, and reduced; yet it's also tangible, audible, has an odor, temperature, texture. It can be simple, or complex, *but it's mostly defined by periodic repetition, by its echo.*

Thematic interpretation is more than just the *subject* of your talk, or the casual or even formal topic of a conversation, it's the unifying "big idea" that pulls it all together, the dominant motif, the great melody that you can't get out of your head once you hear it, the message from God written with fire on stone tablets, or the enlightenment that came to Siddhartha while he rested in the shade of the Bodhi tree after discovering that the cause of human suffering is greed, selfishness, and stupidity.

The theme's like a great river that becomes everything it touches, but never loses its self. It flows to, through, and around, but stays true to its watery essence. We're mostly water, and the blood flowing through our arteries and veins is like the rivers and streams of the greater world around us. Within us there's no beginning, no end, just a continuous flow to and from the heart, a circulatory system more complex, and richer than the Nile, the Ganges, the Thames, the Mekong, the Seine, the Amazon, or the Mississippi.

Thematic interpretation is more than "tying it all together," it's a way to galvanize your program, unleash its vitality, and most important of all, to provide—like all rivers and streams do when they're quiet—moments of transcendent reflection that can last a lifetime.

National parks, and other protected lands, are realms where we can all pause, consider, and dream. When you rest in the shade of the largest trees on earth, or walk at the edge of the grandest canyon in the world, or stop to feel the warm mist of a geyser falling on your face, you're literally in the mood for a grand theme to take you deeper, but for that you need a map, a strategy, *a guide.*

Jon Kohl has provided that guide. He has taken his bearings, mapped out the route, and compass in hand, he's leading the way to a Wonderland. Don't settle for the creek over the hill, or the muddy stream out back. Discover the *Big Idea* that's sitting in the dark like a pearl before the dawn, and use that pearl to illuminate your voyage down the Nile, or the Mississippi. Great works of art have great themes. Great interpretive programs *must* have great themes too. If you work in a protected place that has been set aside by a nation's government, you're probably exploring a setting rich with great themes.

Freeman Tilden has a chapter in *Interpreting Our Heritage* with the title, "The Story's the Thing." Well, at the heart of every great story there's a great theme. What would Mark Twain's seminal American novel *Huckleberry Finn* be without the Mississippi River? Jon Kohl has recognized that fact in the book you're about to read, and the journey you're about to take. There aren't a lot of books out there on *thematic interpretation*, books that teach you how to write strong themes. With a potent theme, you, the interpreter can better stay on course, the visitor has a clearer idea where we're all going, and there's the dramatic tension of obtaining that goal. Again, with this

SHELTON JOHNSON

The Merced River meanders beneath the
Sentinel Bridge in Yosemite Valley

11

book, Jon has provided both map and compass to discovering the heart of thematic interpretation.

Dr. Sam Ham has influenced the thinking of interpreters all over the world, including Jon Kohl and myself. Jon's book is more practical than philosophical, but that's because it's a field guide. Yet it's impossible to communicate the importance of developing good themes in your interpretive programs *without* illuminating those philosophical undercurrents. Consequently, this is a book that every interpreter should have in her or his backpack when they're on the job. Creating a strong theme is the single most important thing you can do to design a program that not only provokes people intellectually and spiritually; but ultimately *moves* people emotionally.

It is those individuals throughout history that have sparked social, artistic, independence, revolutionary, religious, and spiritual movements all around the world, all involved in changing the world by *moving* the world to a different place, a more just and humane space, by forging a new path for our shared planet.

The Nile, the Ganges, the Thames, the Mekong, the Seine, the Amazon, or the Mississippi, are some of the arteries that circulate water, the most magical of elements, throughout a living, breathing earth, the hydrosphere. The surface of the earth is mostly water, and that central theme flows to, around, and through every other story.

Crafting the right theme is no different than connecting parks in a city, or a mountain trail through the wilderness. There's a definite beginning, and an end to be sure, but the real enchantment, like any journey, is along the way where you're occasionally stopped cold in your tracks by beauties strung out like pearls, and even though your body eventually moves on, the memories keep holding on like roots.

In the *Interpretive Theme Writer's Field Guide* Jon Kohl shows us that great themes are not born, *they're made*. Here's how…

Shelton Johnson
U.S. National Park Ranger
Yosemite National Park
U.S. National Park Service

Need for Interpretive Theme Writing Support

My introduction to interpretive themes occurred at the turn of the millennium when I attended a Certified Interpretive Guide workshop. Coming from a background in exhibit development and theater production, I realized that the idea of a unifying vision in a communicative exchange struck a chord. Sam Ham's *Environmental Interpretation* supplied the starting point for my journey of discovery. His later work, *Interpretation: Making a Difference on Purpose,* supplied the research, real-world examples, and practical guidelines that filled my head with possibilities. The implications of his observation that "75 percent of the effort to develop a TORE-quality (Thematic, Organized, Relevant, Enjoyable) interpretive product goes into creating the T itself" opened a conceptual window: interpretive themes are more than literary exercises, they are the distilled manifestation of interpreters' work, reflecting their understanding of both their subject and the people with whom they engage. In short, the development of interpretive themes provides structure and imposes mental discipline. As someone enamored with interpretive theory, I was in high-cotton.

Then I started leading interpretive trainings and reality crashed in. Not everybody has the luxury of time or inclination to wallow in theory. In a training scenario, the instructor can supply coaching. They can lead exercises utilizing worksheets that introduce the concept of themes, opening the door and pointing the direction but the art of interpretation requires constant practice outside of the training oasis. In situations that range from highly supportive to complete isolation, practitioners must take what they have been taught and make it work. The question then was where can they turn for practical guidance that bridges the gap between that one-page worksheet and complex communication theory? Where can they find landmarks when they are unsure of their way? Where is the atlas, the how-to manual? That is what this *Field Guide* is about. It is a quick reference, a map of the byways, a reminder of principles. Hopefully, it will be a helpful companion as you journey down the road of thematic interpretation.

About the Think Tank

In March of 2015, a member of the Certified Interpretive Trainers Network Facebook Group made a great suggestion: "We need a Theme Writing Think Tank page to bounce ideas and get feedback and help." That shared thought led directly to the creation of another Facebook group, the Interpretive Theme Writing Think Tank. This second group is meant to be a safe and supportive playground to kick around ideas on the nature of thematic interpretation and the art of composing effective interpretive themes. While activity has ebbed and flowed, the result is a repository of discussions, documents, and related material providing advice on the use and development of interpretive themes and sharing insights into nature of interpretation. Anyone who is active in the field of heritage interpretation is invited to participate.

Do you have someone you can share your work with, bounce around ideas? As the British writer, comedian, and former Monty Python member John Cleese has said,

> I think it's easy to be creative if you've got other people to play with. I always find that if two or more of us throw ideas backwards and forwards I get to more interesting and original places than I could have ever have gotten to on my own.

This is where the Interpretive Theme Writing Think Tank might prove helpful. It is a venue to share your work and ideas to get feedback from others working in our field. As with all communities, its value is determined by its members' activity. Whether it is the Think Tank or some other venue, find a place you can play with others. Open a doorway, and go on in. You are invited to join the conversation.

Clark Hancock
Creator and Moderator of the Interpretive Theme Writing Think Tank
www.facebook.com/groups/themethinktank
NAI Certified Interpretive Trainer

Who Uses This *Field Guide* and How

As Sam has often noted, the communication discipline we call interpretation enjoys many professional followers who don't even know they are interpreters, such as naturalists, museum curators, environmental educators, protected area managers, advertisers, lawyers, History Channel documentarians, clergy, and of course, military generals. So, this *Field Guide* in theory would be useful not just for frontline interpreters, interpretive planners, and managers, but all these communicators who facilitate deeper appreciations and richer relationships between audience (aka market, clientele, congregation, or army) and heritage, be it person, place, thing, or idea, wherever it occurs.

The theme-writing enthusiast can reap the rewards of this *Field Guide* without ever reading Sam's books. Pity for him or her, though, since those publications reign supreme for professional interpretation development, especially the second, which defines the research pillars upon which interpretation squarely stands. That book delves into detail about the underlying theory and also builds its bibliography. This *Field Guide* on the other hand does not repeat that accomplishment and only briefly mentions theory enough to understand covered techniques. Otherwise it persistently directs you, the reader, to his books and other references as necessary.

Given its role as pocket companion to *Interpretation*, the *Field Guide* serves rather as a how-to and field—not literary—reference guide. I have designed it to accompany you to the field, where your mind and creativity can most readily energize from the inspirational power of ancient temples, leaping waterfalls, enigmatic paintings, crouching tigers, hidden dragons, and other evidence along the creative journey of evolution. I offer many strong theme examples, quotations from famous writers and philosophers about themes, and definitions, and I highlight techniques in the Theme Spotlights. The *Field Guide* contains note-taking space on nearly all of its pages, an Interpretive Theme Writer's Worksheet, a team-based round robin theme-writing worksheet, as well as an "Oh My" page for your most scintillating themes. In addition, most interpretive stations in this guide challenge you with exercises to hone your skills as well as Field Notes with additional tools such as Sam's active verb list from interpretation and recommended reading if, by the end of this training, your appetite to excel remains unsated.

If you prefer to avoid the solitude of writing alone, the *Field Guide* encourages you to theme write in teams or even to facilitate community-based interpretive frameworks. In any case, you do not hike the interpretive stations once, rather you return time and again to its tips, references, and worksheets until you have dominated theme writing and can then confidently gift the guide to some freshman theme writer.

In summary, the objective of the *Field Guide* is clear: Assist communicators in crafting strong interpretive themes in individual, team-, and community-based scenarios, depending on needs and conditions, for the improvement of the craft of heritage interpretation, indeed communication in general, and ultimately promote heritage management and conservation.

The interpretive theme of the *Interpretive Theme Writer's Field Guide* requires more time to process. But I will give you a running start: Crafting a strong interpretive theme should not occur in isolation, rather be a social process involving a wider context and many minds. Furthermore, the lack of a strong and engaging theme development process condemns a communicator to capture an audience's attention and earn its satisfaction through emotional appeals, gimmicks, tricks, and information saturation, most of which fail to provoke or, if they do, will do so poorly in random and likely unrepeatable ways. Better just to develop a strong theme from the get-go!

THEME SPOTLIGHT: THEME OF THEMES

Theme: My culture conditions me to experience myself as separate from everyone and everything else—indeed, I am a single, self-aware being floating untethered in space; but strong interpretive themes can re-connect our separate selves to higher truths about humanity and nature so that we may sew ourselves back into the fabric of the evolving universe.

Technique: Themes, like all concepts, can be interpreted and that's precisely what this *Field Guide* does. This example, while not a conventional format (for example, it uses both first-person singular and plural voices), emphasizes how theme writers shoot for a Big Idea that provokes people to think about their being and place in the universe.

What *Is* Thematic Interpretation, Anyway? And What Is It *Not*?

Interpretation is not the arrow for every target. Some communicators want only to convey information for the enjoyment of their audience or information that makes clear both rules and consequences if violated. Other times, communicators may have well-defined education goals, while others lurk in theme parks seeking nothing more than pure unadulterated entertainment. (In fact, we shouldn't call DisneyLand or Jurassic Park "theme parks" at all—they should be "topic parks.") Other communication branches include social marketing (use of marketing techniques to change social behavior), public relations (to improve the public image or perception of organizations and people), statements of will ("Save the rainforest!"), propaganda (to modify beliefs and behavior through information that can be misleading and deceptive), education (knowledge acquisition and skill development), orientation (helping people find their way), academic publishing (to advance science through the rules of academia), and even small talk among lovers (to strengthen personal relationships).

I mention these forms because if interpreters confuse the kind of communication they wish to engage, their resulting themes only radiate that confusion outward to the audience. Often statements they write aren't interpretive at all. As Sam writes, "When you know ahead of time what you're trying to accomplish, succeeding is much more likely."

Developing the right theme, message, or statement for the situation anchors all communication, not just interpretation, and thus you cannot take this writing task lightly, though some might see it simply as another box to fill in on some obligatory lesson plan format passed down from your boss. If your game is indeed interpretation (see Sam's Chapter 3 on interpretation endgames), then developing the discipline to finely craft a provocative theme marks the difference between a bazooka and a sniper. A sharp, precise theme laser guides the selection of your content and helps visitors to decipher your communication goals. A theme can also straighten out interpreters who wish to hide from accountability: It obligates them to live up to their communication goals; by being written, it makes their ideas public and ensures that the entire team or even community are on the same page and not working at cross-communication purposes as happens in so many organizations.

The cultivated theme allows interpreters to evaluate their communication or to see if the audience's understanding falls within the intended zone of tolerance (see Sam's Chapter 8). Beverly Serrell, in her book on exhibit labels, says, "A powerful exhibition idea [theme] will clarify, limit, and focus the nature and scope of an exhibition and provide a well-defined goal against which to rate its success."

Sam's subtitle "Making a Difference on Purpose" signals that through proper use of interpretation we can greatly increase over random chance alone the probability of desirable and planned change coming into existence. The interpretive theme represents a first great leap down that trail.

All of this can occur because inside the audience's mind, a strong interpretive theme provokes thought, it excites neurons, and makes the audience want to know what lies behind the theme. It makes them beg for more.

When an interpreter leads an audience into an opportunity that provokes thought and emotion that in turn forges connections between the experience and background of the audience with the (not inherent) qualities and meanings of a heritage place or idea, the audience deepens its immediate appreciation and relationship. In that state of heightened awareness, people become, at least temporarily, much more likely to participate if given a convenient means to do so, be it engagement, donations, volunteerism, or something else. Help them love the heritage, provide them a route to express that love, and they will embrace their connection through their investment of time and treasure. That is the major heritage management connection of interpretation, for which Sam in other publications has demonstrated the research links in this cause-effect-love-contribution chain.

But let's not separate themes from their context. Sam argues that successful thematic interpretation must be TORE (Chapter 2): Thematic, Organized, Relevant, and Entertaining. No coincidence that the theme holds the kickoff position, but alone a theme is not a program, not an exhibit; a theme must be developed (see Theme Spotlight: Theme Writing vs. Theme Development at Station 3).

Make no mistake, without a theme, you likely will not have a measurable, successful program or exhibit. Serrell describes how an exhibit might behave without a big idea or strong interpretive theme to lead it:

> Exhibitions that lack a big idea are very common. And they show it because they are overwhelming, confusing, intimidating, and too complex. There are too many labels, and the texts do not relate to the objects. The labels contain too many different ideas that do not clearly relate to each other. They are hard to grasp. They are typically underutilized—the majority of visitors move through them quickly, stopping at fewer than one-third of the elements…. Without a big idea, the job of the label writer is much more difficult: interpretive text contains fragmented, unrelated facts with emphasis on providing information for the sake of information, not on providing meaningful, useful experiences for the visitor's sake.

Don't go there.

Station 1 Big Ideas

1. Interpretation is but one communication approach and does not suit every purpose.

2. A strong theme makes interpretation accountable and evaluable. It allows an interpreter to judge its success within its intended zone of tolerance. It directs selection of content.

3. Theme is the first ingredient to successful TORE-defined thematic interpretation.

4. Without a theme, interpretive media's ability to communicate can break down.

5. Strong interpretive themes and transformational interpretation can provoke audience actions in favor of heritage management and conservation.

STATION 1 EXERCISES

Answers to station exercises can be found in the Field Notes starting on page 115.

1. Draw a line that links the communication type and its corresponding example.

Kinds of statements	Examples
Information	Please keep on the trails.
Propaganda	This site shows the glory of the Inquisitors over the infidels.
Public Relations	The community has participated in the site's interpretation.
Commercial/Marketing	This is the best example of a medieval dungeon still intact.
Will/Command/Should	This arch was built in three years.
Deception	This tree is over 300 years old (in reality, only 100).

2. Mark the following objectives most related to interpretation and justify your answer.

Objective	Related?	Why?
Students will be able to name the five bird species most commonly seen in this refuge.		
Visitors will contribute to a fund that conserves the site's heritage values.		
Visitors will record "very satisfied" as the average response on a visitor satisfaction survey.		
Visitors will develop a deeper appreciation for why the site's heritage is so important to the community's identity.		
Visitors will be able to explain why parasites are such an important part of ecosystem function.		
Visitors will choose the site as the most entertaining recreational option within the community for Friday nights during the summer season.		
Visitors will not step beyond the protective railing at the crater's edge.		
Visitor restaurant purchases will increase 5 percent annually from the 2018 baseline.		
Students will join the volunteer conservation corps at 10 percent annually from 2018 at the heritage site.		
Retired population will indicate an increase in heritage pride after visiting the site.		

BO MERTZ

THEME SPOTLIGHT: STRONG VS. WEAK THEMES

Weak Theme: Technology alone will not solve climate change.

Strong Theme: As humanity faces a civilization-sized threat in climate change caused by its relationship with a finite planet, technological answers such as switching fossil fuels for alternative sources, will only remedy, not solve, the underlying problem.

Definition: The glossary entry for a strong theme from Sam's book reads that a strong theme is "a theme that is both easy to process and relevant. A strong theme has high provocation likelihood." This is the central definition that we use in this *Field Guide*.

THEME SPOTLIGHT: MESSAGE VS. THEME

Theme: "The illiterate of the 21st Century will not be those who cannot read or write, but those who cannot learn, unlearn, and relearn."

—Alvin Toffler

Definition: Is this a message or a theme? While many people use either word to mean the same thing, rather than use them as synonyms, Sam suggests that "theme" used in the context of music or poetry is an idea that an artist presents and develops in collaboration with his or her audience; while a "message" is that which a communicator wants the audience to understand, perhaps word for word without interpretation, and implicitly to accept and agree.

Pictured above: Here the artist sings a song that provokes the audience into creating meaning associated with this song. In other words, the artist co-develops with the audience the song's meaning or theme.

Theme Notes

We Write Themes for Primary and Secondary Audiences

When you stand in front of a group of visitors eager to experience your opening words, you may feel a little doubt about who your audience is, about which demographics lurk behind smiling faces. Often, that very same image of a visitor gaze trained on you can haunt your theme-writing mind when your fingers first dance on a keyboard ready to craft a theme. It can cloud judgment and overshadow important theme-writing criteria. In fact, experts too can forget for whom they write their themes. You might have spotted these example themes taken from published books about interpretation:

- Toads lead a double life that may amaze you.

- There are many ways you can help protect this historic park.

- A healthy swamp—an example of a threatened ecosystem—provides many surprising benefits to humans.

- Birds take flight for life.

Experts often argue that themes must give direction to presentations, which implies that they serve interpreters in the construction of interpretive presentations. Yet these experts may still offer "model" examples written to be read by or orally presented to that eager audience. (I infer these examples are intended for direct use because the first two examples use "you." The third example uses "surprising" without saying what those surprises are, thus functioning as a teaser. The last has sacrificed clarity for poetry, a quality, one must suppose, meant to provoke an attentive audience.) Yet none of these book authors specify the audience or else they simply assume the audience to be the visiting public. Or they assume that the theme serves equally well for both audience and interpreter.

As Sam points out in Chapter 9, sometimes you do write themes to be revealed directly word-for-word to your audiences (what he calls the "sandwich" and "emergent" models versus the "implicit" model so common in fiction). Other times, perhaps most of the time, you write the theme only for yourself, the interpreter, as a planning tool. Whichever model you choose depends on your communication objectives.

It's fair to say that if you haven't clearly considered your strategy or whether the audience is you or the visitor, your resulting theme may well fail to meet your objectives. Consider these unfortunate scenarios:

- You prepare a program on birds and consider only an audience of birders. You try to appeal to them without applying your own criteria and you end up with a factual bird theme rather than one with a Big Idea.

- You write a theme about indigenous cosmologies and people tell you to drop it because it is not appropriate for children.

- You write a theme designed for a poor school in the mountains. You think it might appeal to them, but you don't really like it. You never get enthused and in the end your lack of inspiration shows on the children's straight faces.

- You are hired as an interpretive consultant to do an interpretive plan. You write a great theme in your opinion but none of the local stakeholders relate to its greatness, and they never use it.

- Alternatively, you allow the community to write it, they get really excited even though it is a purely factual statement about their community. You know that international tourists will sigh ho-hum. But because it is the local folks' creation, you collude with them to keep it as written.

To help theme writers navigate this meaning minefield, we distinguish between primary and secondary audiences. You will find this distinction on the Interpretive Theme Writer's Worksheet in the Field Notes at the back of this guide.

Primary Audience

The primary audience embodies the person (for example, you) or people who originally create the theme, who "own" it in the sense of identifying personally with its creation. The primary audience may be a single interpreter, an interpretive team, a wider internal staff, or an entire heritage community. However many people comprise the primary audience, we can apply Sam's advice that if you (the primary audience) are not inspired by your own theme, don't expect anyone else to be either. You are the very first filter applied to the new-borne thematic being. Thus, the author(s) of the themes must first write it for him/her/them/ourselves to ensure its inspirational power; it should—to use Sam's high bar—provoke goose bumps of excitement.

In other words, the primary audience fortifies the theme with Vitamin R or relevance because the theme reflects your own experience and knowledge, meets personal or institutional objectives, and provokes thought. Once your theme has met your own criteria, now the question is, do we rewrite it for a secondary audience?

Secondary Audience

For every primary audience, at least one secondary audience stands eagerly in anticipation of the interpretive opportunity. But in most cases, every primary audience serves a variety of secondary audiences and most likely none of them will react to the primary theme with the same unbridled enthusiasm. Thus, the primary audience or authors of the interpretive theme may need to adapt their primary theme to the secondary audience, effectively creating secondary themes that prove more relevant for that particular audience. This is true whether you intend to show the theme directly or not to that audience, because it manifests in how the interpreter mentally prepares for an interpretive interaction. As Sam says, theme writing is highly audience dependent.

> I think what "The Hobbit" and Middle-earth deal in are quite universal and timeless themes of honour and love and friendship... so they're things that do resonate with people.
>
> *Martin Freeman*

Now the secondary theme may be worded with lesser or greater legibility, more or less complexity, make references to the particular background of the secondary audience, but it should always retain the essence of the primary theme. Otherwise it runs the risk of becoming a different primary theme entirely. Consider this example:

Primary theme: Two hundred million years of dinosaurian dominance on Earth did not influence naming of geological time periods, while human building and cropping for mere thousands may result in the naming of the Anthropocene Epoch.

Secondary theme for children: Dinosaurs lived a very long time and didn't change the earth. People have been here for a much shorter time. Yet we have changed the oceans, skies, and land. (Fifth-grade level, 10- to 11-year-olds)

Secondary theme for conservationists: Changing geological time periods have been named in part for mass extinctions caused by geological and climatic factors; now, for the first time, the current mass extinction results from a biological factor: the human species.

Secondary theme for birders: The ancestors of birds flew and jumped with other dinosaurs for millions of years during which the geological time period did not change; now after mere millennia of human building and cropping, and the extinction of numerous charismatic bird species, the name may change to the Anthropocene Epoch.

As the primary theme should be relevant and strong for the primary audience, so the secondary theme should achieve the same for the secondary audience.

Which primary themes should I write?

While all themes should wield high provocation power or likelihood (to use Sam's term) whether for primary or secondary audiences, this quality does not limit the topics you can cover (Sam distinguishes between themes and topics in *Environmental Interpretation*). To decide which topics, like seeds, you should plant and cultivate into themes, consider the advice of Lisa Brochu, who argues that the selection of topics and themes depends on the relative importance of three factors: management decisions (i.e., objectives), visitor interest (i.e., audience relevance), and resource stories (i.e., heritage qualities). To this we might add a fourth: the interpreter's own knowledge, preferences, and inspiration. Theme selection must harmonize this quartet.

With respect to management objectives, you select themes related to site purpose, management objectives, and agency orientation. For example, the Valle de Oro National Wildlife Refuge in Albuquerque, New Mexico, wrote an agency-mission theme in addition to those determined by the community: "Valle de Oro extends the gradient of engaging activities that traditional refuges offer right up to the doorstep of every urban dweller, no matter their prior experience with wildlife or its protection." The agency mission overrides visitor interests, but an interpretive framework built from several themes can easily accommodate both kinds of themes in different but complementary doses. If another management objective requires the strengthening of community ownership of managed heritage, then the community becomes a primary audience and itself writes at least one theme. (See Station 7 on how you might facilitate this.)

With respect to visitor interests, you want your set of themes to exude relevance for at least the principal audience segments. You can also derive secondary themes for pretty much any audience. Clearly if you need a theme for a specific program or offering, then your audience is highly specific and you would tailor one of your primary themes to those folks. Don't forget of course that during the actual theme development or presentation you do most of your audience tailoring. It's one thing to tailor a theme that the secondary audience may never see directly, but it's another completely to tailor the presentation to fully tap into the audience's background and experience to make the experience highly thematic, organized, relevant, and entertaining.

With respect to heritage qualities, of course, your site limits your possibilities. If its founding legislation established it for a battlefield, think Gettysburg, you may steer wide of too many natural heritage themes. If a site blends in with surrounding territory ecologically, you may dig for Big Ideas in the site's geology.

And the fourth depends completely on you. Which theme you write also depends on what you know and what provokes your own thoughts.

And Then There Are Sub-themes

Many interpretive planners use the term "sub-themes." This *Field Guide* defines a sub-theme as a component of a larger theme, whether primary or secondary. A sub-theme is not necessarily adapted to a particular audience, rather it describes a component of a larger theme. But like any theme, sub-themes are expressed in complete sentences. See the example in the Theme Spotlight.

Station 2 Big Ideas

1. The primary audience consists of the theme author(s) while the secondary audience represents people who interact with interpretive media.

2. The primary audience writes the primary theme to its own satisfaction and approval. The primary audience then rewrites or derives a secondary theme for the purpose of strengthening its relevance for any given secondary audience (visiting public).

3. Topic or theme selection depends on the interaction of four criteria: management decisions, visitor interests, resources stories, and interpreter knowledge and inspiration.

4. Sub-themes are component themes that integrate into a higher-level theme, whether primary or secondary.

STATION 2 EXERCISE

Answers to station exercises can be found in the Field Notes starting on page 115.

Fill in the table below with the appropriate item from the list.

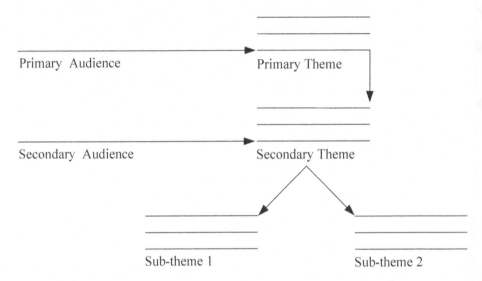

a. Even though more than half of the signers owned slaves and even though the full expression of freedom had not yet occurred, the American Declaration of Independence remains the greatest statement of the innate right of all people to freedom and equality.

b. Interpretive staff at a museum about the underground railroad

c. Slavery in America has been formally abolished in word, but in deed, equal rights for African-Americans and other minorities still must catch up with the lofty aspirations set by the Declaration of Independence.

d. Middle-class American African-Americans

e. Since every country includes people with varying degrees of consciousness, culture wars over slavery and other expressions of human and environmental rights wage such as the American Civil War and its need to smuggle blacks out of the south along the Underground Railroad.

f. In a mere hundred years formal slavery had been abolished the world over as nation states evolved from traditional to modern consciousness which values that all "men" are created equal.

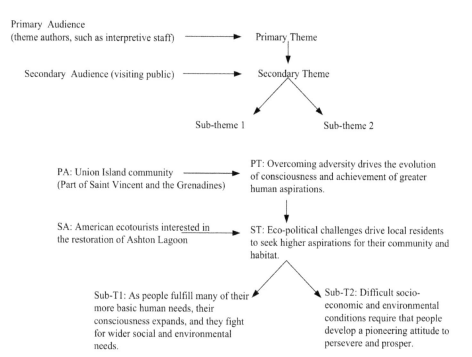

Primary Audience
(theme authors, such as interpretive staff) ⟶ Primary Theme

Secondary Audience (visiting public) ⟶ Secondary Theme

Sub-theme 1   Sub-theme 2

PA: Union Island community ⟶ PT: Overcoming adversity drives the evolution
(Part of Saint Vincent and the Grenadines)   of consciousness and achievement of greater
                                               human aspirations.

SA: American ecotourists interested in ⟶ ST: Eco-political challenges drive local residents
the restoration of Ashton Lagoon   to seek higher aspirations for their community and
                                          habitat.

Sub-T1: As people fulfill many of their   Sub-T2: Difficult socio-
more basic human needs, their   economic and environmental
consciousness expands, and they fight   conditions require that people
for wider social and environmental   develop a pioneering attitude to
needs.   persevere and prosper.

THEME SPOTLIGHT: SECONDARY THEMES VS. SUB-THEMES

Theme: See graphic.

Definition: The primary audience [theme author(s)] writes the primary theme for its own approval and satisfaction. The primary audience then rewrites, if necessary, a secondary theme for a secondary audience (visitors). That secondary theme might be broken down into sub-(secondary) themes. In the figure, we see the real primary audience and theme from a theme creation exercise on Union Island, St. Vincent, and the Grenadines. The secondary audience and theme have been created for this exercise, while the sub-themes come directly from the original interpretive framework.

Theme Notes

Strong Interpretive Themes Embody Big Ideas and Vehicles to Deliver Them

Serrell uses the term "big idea" essentially in the same way this *Field Guide* uses the term "interpretive theme." Here though I use the term "big idea" as the precursor to the interpretive theme because, as Sam points out, the interpretive theme writer must consider other aspects as well to write a theme, such as the use of examples, voice, and readability. Because of these, I separate the concept of Big Idea and the theme itself. You might also see this separation as similar to how inspiration precedes the powerful statement carefully constructed.

> The whole theme of *Interview with the Vampire* was Louis's quest for meaning in a godless world. He searched to find the oldest existing immortal simply to ask, "What is the meaning of what we are?"
>
> *Anne Rice*

As mentioned before, the Big Idea provokes not just streaming thoughts but goosebumps on your arm. In this distinction, we could fairly say that the content of the Big Idea, not the writing itself, makes people think by revealing a new perspective or angle the casts new light on the human condition, how Nature operates, or some similar universal reality. A Big Idea epitomizes the often mentioned concept of universal intangibility (see almost any book on interpretation).

The Big Idea generates this effect because it addresses people's most deeply concerning questions, but not because of clever writing, emotion-laden examples, or tantalizing details that can readily capture attention as any horror movie director knows, but because it unlocks mental doors to elaboration and processing well beyond the initial attention grab. To be fair, attention-grabbing does direct audience attention, a point we will grab at Station 5 about vehicles.

Perhaps a Big Idea relates to organizational learning and business guru Peter Senge's idea of vision. A strong vision, he says, inspires resource mobilization toward the fulfillment of that vision. If resources stay put, the vision has failed. It is useless. A Big Idea like a vision first mobilizes thought and then action if conditions prove appropriate. On a similar note, Ron Berger, Libby Woodfin, and Anne Vilen argue the need for Big Ideas in education. They cite Harvard professor David Perkins who

> reminds us that big ideas and disciplinary frameworks are what allow students to make sense of the facts they encounter. Without these frameworks, it is like giving students a lot of bricks—discrete facts—and asking them to build a house. Without blueprints—big ideas and disciplinary frameworks—all the students have is a pile of bricks. They have no idea how to build understanding with them.

The Vehicle Mobilizes the Big Idea

The vehicle—the refined written theme—gives body to and mobilizes the Big Idea. I use it here in a somewhat broader or evolved way than Sam used the term in *Environmental Interpretation*, as a way to make a topic more interesting. Here, instead of topic, we apply it to Big Ideas. By writing the Big Idea in effective language, the Big Idea can be more readily noticed and quickly integrated into the audience's awareness. Of course, an experienced theme writer can bang out the Big Idea as a strong interpretive theme in the very first draft, endowing it with both relevance and processing ease, which are to say: provocation power or likelihood. But for those who cannot boast of such craftiness may well benefit from first focusing on the Big Idea and then how to mold its form to enhance mental absorbability. The power of vehicle in great measure obeys numerous simple guidelines, which we explore at Station 5; the power of the Big Idea, on the other hand, takes form more from intuition than nicely defined directives.

Thus, this distinction Big Idea–Vehicle is entirely for learning purposes, just as the following analogies to explain it. For example, the distinction reminds me of a NASA space mission. The mission has a vision and objectives that can inspire (the Big Idea) President Kennedy's goal to be the first country to land a man on the moon. But inspiration alone will not suffice if the *Apollo 11* spacecraft (the vehicle) had no lunar module to touch down and see that vision through to its historical conclusion. In other words, getting to space (the job of the space vehicle) is never

THEME SPOTLIGHT: BIG IDEA VS. INTERPRETIVE THEME

Big Idea: Reproduction and spirituality are the same force.

Theme: Sex between people, as well as the spiritual drive to improve the world, are examples of the same creative impulse that has made the universe more complex and mysterious since its beginning: The Big Bang.

Definition: This *Field Guide* distinguishes between the Big Idea and the interpretive theme because you can edit the Big Idea in a number of ways

JUPITER SEDUCING OLYMPIAS / CIRCA 1526

to make it stronger and more appealing, effectively molding the Big Idea into an interpretive theme. Expert theme writers can merge both elements at once. Consider the Big Idea a shaped mound of clay, formed enough to commit the sculptor to a certain direction, who then refines the sculpture eventually to be exhibited.

Please realize that a well-written Big Idea may already be a strong interpretive theme without further need for refinement. For example, had I written the Big Idea as "Reproduction and spirituality come from the same fundamental creative force in the universe," you might justifiably conclude that it is already an interpretive theme without need to improve it with the example theme above.

Indeed, if everyone could write strong themes the first time around, there would be no need for this distinction. And no doubt at times throughout this *Field Guide,* you will indeed see their use as interchangeable, while in other instances, their difference you will also see as necessary.

This Big Idea comes from spiritual teacher Andrew Cohen who defines the Evolutionary Impulse in the universe. Though he has often talked about various forms that this impulse takes, he has not crafted it into a formal interpretive theme for programming. See this short video on the topic here: https://youtu.be/ARpws5Sjwc

the mission. Rather the mission is to explore, seek out new forms of life and civilizations, boldly go where no man has gone before… (that's a Big Idea!). But if the vehicle doesn't work properly, even a small O Ring malfunction can terminate the mission (which might be equivalent to using a "prohibited word" that hides rather than reveals the meaning or Big Idea.

Another metaphor might be a helper protein—the vehicle—that guides a nutrient like glucose across the blood-brain-barrier so that it can be absorbed and incorporated into brain cells rather than blocked and discarded.

Thus, the Big Idea eclipses in importance the vehicle, at least, by a little. Since the audience almost never constructs its meaning the way the interpreter did, the actual writing or construction of the theme isn't mission critical, except on occasions when the interpreter demands a narrow zone of tolerance (Chapter 8) and shares the theme directly as written with the audience (Chapter 9).

Even with a Big Idea, if not delivered by an effective vehicle, the audience may not feel compelled to pay attention or even contemplate the idea at all. The risk then for the novice theme writer is the manufacture of a theme embellished with clever wording, impeccable economy, poetic pedigree that ultimately fails to stimulate the synergistic melody of harmonic thought. So much sound and fury signifying nothing!

Likewise, the opposite can occur with pre-Big Ideas. If you cannot express them, they are nothing more than inaccessible feelings, nebulous thoughts, and incoherent intuitions that you cannot communicate clearly to an audience. To avoid suffering either of these unceremonious finales, we say that theme strength integrates both the Big Idea and vehicle, the ying and yang, the provocation and ease of processing.

Station 3 Big Ideas

1. A Big Idea connects people to their deepest questions.

2. A vehicle gives the Big Idea form such that the audience is more likely to notice the Big Idea and think about it.

3. While a Big Idea can generate horsepower without the vehicle, a vehicle without a Big Idea is little more than a gimmick.

Aside from writing a theme for his dinosaur talk, this guide also had to develop it when he selected his visual aids and objects.

THEME SPOTLIGHT: THEME WRITING VS. THEME DEVELOPMENT

Theme: The only distinction between World Heritage and everything else are the meanings that we assign.

Definition: Sam distinguishes between theme writing and theme development as two separate and sequential tasks. Theme writers (whether individuals or community groups) work behind the scenes to write their themes, out of sight of the visiting public. After the writing, they must craft and express their themes in actual programs, signage, exhibitions, and other interpretive media. To develop the theme, they select objects, write text, practice presentations, edit video, etc. They apply most of their skills in interpretation during theme development.

In communication, when we say 'develop' a theme, we mean to flesh it out, give it substance, and put meat on its bones. In other words, in developing a theme, interpreters now bring to the forefront carefully selected facts, points of interest, universal concepts, tangible-intangible connections, anecdotes, analogies, examples, metaphors, and other forms of 'color' to make theme resonate for the audience." —Sam Ham

STATION 3 EXERCISE

Answers to station exercises can be found in the Field Notes starting on page 115.

Identify Big and Small Ideas and Justify Your Choice.

Idea	Size	Why?
Continuous war for centuries precipitated union in Europe.		
Big countries co-exist with small countries in Europe.		
Supra-national self-identity in the European Union generates more advanced ethical values.		
Several common languages bind the many countries of the European Union.		
People simultaneously act with a sense of national identity as well as European identity and this is not only acceptable but promoted across the continent.		
There are almost as many countries in Europe (51) as there are in Africa (55).		

THEME SPOTLIGHT: THEMES SHOULD PRESENT AN ARGUMENT

Themes: Despite the crowds that throng the valley floor, Yosemite is a "de-peopled" landscape.

We often think of wilderness as a geographical place, but time is also a wilderness.

Technique: These examples come from a 1997 *Legacy* article by Ann Lundberg in which she argues that what we call themes in this *Field Guide* should present an argument to provoke people's thinking. She offers the following characteristics of a good "thesis" or interpretive theme (when she says "theme" she means factual statement):

Sam Ham makes the argument for interpretation at the international interpretation conference in Panama.

- Expresses the goal of your presentation.
- Suggests a point of view you will convince the audience to accept.
- Presents an argument that directs the route by which you will prove your case.
- Provokes, stimulates, and inspires the audience to actively participate in the reasoning process of your program.
- Is personal, based on your own experience and understanding of the material you are addressing, which no one else could produce.
- Takes a risk. If you have nothing to lose, you have nothing to gain.
- Is more complex, with a more complex sentence structure than a theme.
- Connects your theme to the larger picture, suggesting how it affects the wider range of the audience's experience, including what they will do or think tomorrow.

Sam invited Larry Beck and Ted Cable (see his "Last Word" at the end of this *Field Guide*) to respond to Ann's article in *Interpretation: Making a Difference on Purpose* (p. 109).

THEME SPOTLIGHT: THEME = OBJECT + BIG IDEA

Theme:
- Object (topic) = Anthropocene
- Idea = The time may be right to rename our geological epoch.
- Theme = Due to human modification of planetary systems, the time may be right to rename our current geological epoch as the Anthropocene.

Definition: We often read about how a theme should connect tangible and intangible elements; another way to say this is that you have some object to be interpreted (also known as a topic), whether person, place, thing, or idea, and then you have a Big Idea that relates to it, comments on it, opines about it. An object alone is an incomplete sentence. A Big Idea alone would be philosophy and not interpretation. We must have both.

Pictured above: A cement plant breaks up the landscape
outside of Chagres National Park, Panama, and provides
evidence of why we now survive in the Anthropocene.

Theme Notes

Interpreters Must Ignite Their Inspiration for the Big Idea, Not Just Write It

You, I, and all people create meaning from the moment we are born (some suggest earlier) to the moment we die (others suggest later), while sleeping and awake. Our meaning-making psychological drive marches onward, unstoppable.

When we face life's threats, this drive generates ideas that help us to survive. "Necessity is the mother of invention." But when we largely live without threats, the meaning-making process may not focus. Such as when we walk through a heritage area, all sorts of ideas may enter our heads, our minds might wander, connecting to random facets of experience, positive and negative attitudes, any kind of stimuli, reinforcing misconceptions. This survival instinct to create meaning evolved over eons. But in whatever moment, the right conditions must exist, the stage must be set, to best take advantage of this inherently human power.

> I never try to convey a message, I just want to tell a story. Why that story in particular? I have no idea, but I have learned to surrender to the muse. I become obsessed with a theme or with certain stories; they haunt me for years, and finally, I write them.
>
> *Isabel Allende*

As communicators we guide that force in non-threat situations, bring temporary order, give it purpose, to accelerate understanding of the world around us, so that it serves the heritage we aim to protect. To live without meaning often ends in death. Consider people and cultures that have lost their meaning, crushed by hard times, colonialists, or conquerors such as the Mayans whose sacred codices (books) were destroyed by the Spanish or more recently Syrians whose millennial heritage, like the World Heritage ancient city of Palmyra, was smashed by ISIS.

A Big Idea is Critical

A great speaker can attribute her greatness only partially to oratory skill, and partially because she has something critical to say—a Big Idea. If you have seen a TED.com talk, you understand the centrality of a Big Idea; TED's tagline is "Ideas worth spreading." Interpretation's inspiration and transformation power emanates from the Big Idea. During our normal interactions, we hear Big Ideas all the time, some repeatedly. Some we call aphorisms, sayings, proverbs, most of which share some universal wisdom.

1. "We do not see things as they are; we see things as we are." —The Talmud

2. "We become just by performing just actions, temperate by performing temperate actions, brave by performing brave actions." —Aristotle

3. "The world we have created is a product of our thinking; it cannot change without changing our thinking." —Albert Einstein

4. "Material abundance without character is the path of destruction." —Thomas Jefferson

5. "There is no greater agony than bearing an untold story inside you." —Maya Angelou

The opposite of the Big Idea is cliché, hackneyed and tired, easily verified facts, the difference between cocaine and a tic tac. To illustrate this, let's look at example Big Ideas which are not yet written up with vehicles (see above discussion of "vehicle").

Big Idea about Big Ideas: Big Ideas move culture forward, opening up new avenues of individual and societal growth, often accompanied by conflict.

Heritage: There is no difference between natural and cultural heritage; there is only one process of evolution that creates heritage. People draw these arbitrary lines of distinction.

Person: No person is a random historical event, rather a product of intersecting social forces. Trained as a lawyer, Abraham Lincoln, for the South, served as judge, jury, and executioner for a new chapter in American freedom.

Concept: Despite that more than half the framers owned slaves, the *US Declaration of Independence* more than any other document declared the basic principles of an emerging human equality. Neil Armstrong uttered another Big Idea: "One small step for man, one giant leap for mankind."

More Big Ideas from the book *Learning that Lasts:*

- The meaning of artifacts depends on who owns them and who tells their story.

- Enduring civilizations have stable and productive economies that allow for the accumulation of wealth.

> You can't tell any kind of a story without having some kind of a theme, something to say between the lines.
>
> *Robert Wise*

- Physical geography influences the characteristics and success or decline of civilizations.

- The way material behaves depends on how its atoms are arranged.

- Correlation in data is not the same as causation in data.

We now understand that the Big Idea is no interpretive formality to be simply checked off. The Big Idea must provoke curiosity, fascination, and ignite, as Sam likes to say, a fire in the belly. An ordinary idea won't do. The difference between an ordinary idea and a Big Idea is the difference between a match in a box and a match in ignition. The pinnacle of an interpreter's work must be when a visitor actually transforms his or her worldview in a way that alters outlook and behavior permanently.

As discussed at the last station, a step prior to visitor enlightenment requires first that the theme fire up passion and inspiration in the primary audience which then increases the chances of doing the same in the secondary. But interpreters like anyone whose pursuits depend on creativity cannot simply sit back and wait for inspiration to knock at the door. You must do the work. You must identify in your own personal way how to tap into a creative, inspirational force. You must call upon that force as does the master of a genie bottle. Ask any writer or painter what they do. There is no formula, but fortunately there are techniques that may help to ignite your own inspiration to reveal Big Ideas, techniques that may be a light to you in dark places when all other lights go out.

Researching Your Topic Is a Good Place to Start

Let's start with the obvious. Research your topic (or "object" as mentioned in the previous theme spotlight). The goal isn't to become a content expert necessarily (although that almost never hurts), rather as your research progresses you may expose yourself to provocative new perspectives about your topic. This requires of course that you read widely. During this research journey you may read someone else's Big Idea or the readings may spark your own. Either will do. The journey also carries the assumption that you have thought deeply about your topic and what it means to you. As Sam advises, "A professional has to show up and do their job and has to write competently strong themes when necessary. But granted they will do even better if they write about something that matters to them." It is also important to not limit your search to a single point-of-view or to information that only supports your particular prejudice. Remember to be open. You will develop your own understanding but by investigating various perspectives, you provide yourself with essential knowledge for guiding others from their starting point.

Another way to understand the effect of research: Wide-ranging research can result in a constellation of perspectives and facts a few of which you can sew together to create yet newer associations and perspectives that tie your topic into other universal topics. "Wide-ranging" ideally means that you read well beyond your topic itself, as often the richest connections occur between your topic and a completely different and seemingly unrelated topic, later revealed to be connected in a previously invisible and perhaps mysterious way. This advice only produces results after years of insatiable curiosity which characterizes the very best, well-rounded, worldly interpreters.

Being a "content expert" alone, if unaccompanied by this curiosity that crosses disciplinary boundaries like migrating hawks cross state lines is not very useful for interpretation. It can close the mind and cut off connections. Doing or studying something a long time (often called "experience") can have two effects on your mindset: It can open your mind to new perspectives and possibilities or cement it in old and unchanging ideas. We've all heard of the stuffy old professor who uses the same teaching notes from 30 years ago. This is a person for whom the fount of inspiration has dried up a long time ago, someone for whom the term "experience" doesn't quite fit.

Inspiration can explode into your consciousness like fireworks in the sky. Indeed, for Johannes Brahms, that seemed to be his pathway to success: "Straight-away the ideas flow in upon me, directly from God, and not only do I see distinct themes in my mind's eye, but they are clothed in the right forms, harmonies, and orchestration." But most of us don't enjoy that kind of synchronicity with the universe. More likely inspiration takes the form of a glimpse that requires significant time to tease out and finally name. Serrell makes this point: "It takes time. Hours, days, even months. It's not a matter of just wordsmithing. It takes a lot of thinking and rethinking. It is messy. There's lots of editing and reediting. Starting over. Sleeping on it…." She gives an example of one Big Idea that took 50 hours and lots of conversations among the exhibit design team to develop. For an exhibit, Big Idea selection is a big decision, one that can cost a lot of money.

Do not be tempted to stop before a truly Big Idea has been completely unearthed or be unwilling to continually revisit the Big Idea. All professional writers know the temptation but also know that they must keep editing and rewriting to distill the Big Idea and the strong theme that follows. My textbook on heritage interpretation had versions running into the upper teens for each chapter.

> Genius is one percent inspiration and 99 percent perspiration.
> *Thomas Edison*

Someone once pointed out to me the common experience of students who write a research paper and in writing their conclusion, their main idea or thesis finally becomes clear to them, like a ray of sun beaming through an ominous storm cloud. For those who pursue excellence, they grab that idea, move it to the front of the paper, call it their thesis, and then revise the whole work. For those who just want to finish, they leave their topic idea trapped in the conclusion where it contributes not at all to the structure, argument, or reader experience. The same applies to theme writing if you accept mediocrity or a little idea rather than track the hints and glints that guide you down a golden brick path to the Big Idea.

Different Approaches to Igniting the Inspiration

Hopefully one of the following techniques will ignite your inspiration.

Grammatical Approach

In 1992, Sam proposed this simple approach in *Environmental Interpretation*. Complete the following sentence and you will have a candidate Big Idea: "After having heard my presentation (read my exhibition, etc.), I want my audience to understand that…."

Example: "A graveyard, much more than a respectable space to dispose of the deceased, concentrates spiritual meaning into a sacred, inhabited place." The Grammatical Approach alone is unlikely to get you where you want to be. Consider another approach proposed by Sam.

Big Deal Approach

Complete this sentence: "After the visitors have spent the entire day in our park, walked our trails, read our information, viewed our signs, talked with our staff, and are now just leaving, possibly never to return, if they remember and understand just one message or idea about the park, after everything they have done and seen

THEME SPOTLIGHT:
CONNECTING UNLIKE POINTS TO CAST NEW LIGHT

Theme: The collapse of human civilizations is not a history of slowly degrading ability to provide basic services, but a long ignorance of society's decline by its leaders.

Definition: Often the best themes come from the connection of perspectives from different fields of thought. Finding similarity in the haystack of apparent dissimilarity often provokes pleasant surprises. In this case, the first half of the theme could have been written by someone who studies collapse from a geographical or sociological perspective while the second comes more from a political science perspective.

Pictured above: Ruins of a Native American community in Chaco Culture National Historic Park may hide clues to its collapse.

here, this message that they absolutely have to understand is that…."

Example: "Drought doesn't just alter plant and animal communities, but may even alter the very identity of the place itself."

Deep Meaning Approach
Follow these steps.

1. Describe the object to be interpreted. The remote control is black and has blue and purple number buttons, is made by the RCA company, and measures 30 centimeters.

2. Ask why and what. Why is it black? Why did RCA elect to make a remote control at all? What kind of plastic is it?

3. Answer the more interesting questions, and toss the others. (Since I have not done research on RCA remote controls, the following answers are fabricated for educational purposes.) The black color is part of a recent fad in electronics, perhaps reminiscent of Darth Vader. It is short so that it can be held along with a can of pop in the same hand. RCA made the remote so that we would not have to get up to change the TV channel, so that we can continue to honor the art of laziness.

4. Identify the important or meaningful idea. Certainly, by not having to get up, the average viewer gains weight. Some controls don't just control channels anymore; now you can manage the stereo, lights, and garage door too, all from the comfort of your sofa.

5. Choose the best idea. What else does not getting up from the sofa mean to American society? (Now we are talking more universal than the remote itself.) Maybe remote controls are early precursors to the computerization of smart houses. Remote controls symbolize our society's desire for convenience at any cost, whether money, activity, or even health. Or maybe it symbolizes status and wealth as poor people without the luxury of remote controls have to get up and move around despite their best intentions.

6. Write the Big Idea or even the strong theme. "The remote control represents the transformation of the American living room by the couch-centered leisure industry into middle-class society's final resting place."

Five Whys/So What (Socratic) Approach
This approach works even better if you have someone who can serve as your foil or student, like Sherlock Holmes did with John Watson or Socrates with his students. Ask the question "Why?" or "So what?" five times, each time going deeper, closer to root causes, where real meaning lurks. Usually you start with an interesting fact: The song of a humpback whale can be heard by other whales thousands of kilometers away.

Why 1? The underwater realm is very large and visibility is poor so this is the only way they can find each other.

Why 2? Because they don't have psychic ability or any other mechanism to otherwise communicate.

Why 3? Their brains have not developed extra-sensory powers.

Why 4? Because evolution has chosen to develop the hardware and software needed to communicate sonically, although it could have used perhaps chemical signals like so many other creatures do in the ocean.

Why 5? Evolution chooses pathways to successful adaptation but that does not mean that other pathways couldn't have worked as well such as chemical signaling or telepathy.

Theme: When organisms face challenges, evolution selects for successful solutions that do not exclude other possible solutions as well, such as humpback whales that communicate over thousands of kilometers with audible songs rather than, for instance, chemical signals or telepathy.

Evolutionary Forces Approach
This approach works by understanding how something has come to be, how it fits into the evolutionary stream. Ultimately everything in the universe is the result of evolution and how things came to be (and where they are going) is the fundamental source of meaning from traditional creation-based stories to post-modern spiritual universal stories and everywhere in between. You can understand all heritage elements as markers along this evolutionary path; every evolutionary adaptation leaves behind clues to its passage. Even the Big Bang 14.5 billion years ago left evidence in the form of background microwave radiation still detectable today.

Van Matre in his 2008 book on interpretation explains that universal forces and processes combine energy, material, and (according to the observations of systems thinker Donella Meadows) objectives to create unique features or products (our heritage). Understanding those universal processes behind tangible heritage gives us a much deeper understanding and appreciation for the heritage and the processes.

1.   Choose an object to be interpreted.

2.   Ask: What processes and forces created it?

3.   Ask: What are the materials, energy, and objectives that bind it together?

4.   Ask: What does this tell us about evolution itself and how the object fits into the universe?

5.   Write your Big Idea.

Example:

1.   Diamonds

2.   Pressure from other rocks, gravity, time

3.   Carbon + pressure from other rocks + gravity + time + self-organization

4.   Even the hardest of materials are subject to change; the universe in all its forms constantly changes.

5.   Different minerals, like diamonds, emerge from the evolving complexity of Earth, born of space dust and energy.

Irony Revelation Approach
One of my favorite techniques seeks irony through words like "despite," "although," "on the other hand," "though," etc. It contrasts what people commonly understand (depends on the audience, of course) with what you want to reveal behind the common understanding. The clash between the two should provoke sparks, thought. The approach arises from the notion that every object, both material and immaterial, can be observed from multiple perspectives. Even time itself is relative. Most people, nonetheless, see most things from one perspective, typically the dominant one in their circle. That perspective or belief, then, is your target. That perspective you aim to challenge with this interpretive approach.

1.   Choose that dominant belief about your interpreted object.

2.   Start a sentence with a word that indicates contrast or irony: Despite, although, even though, while, however…

3.   State or write the common perspective.

4.   Choose an entirely different way to observe that same object.

5.   In the second half of the sentence, reveal the new perspective or the irony about

the same object. For example: Despite that geology is the study of rocks, the current geological period may be renamed based on human not geologic activity.

Freewriting Approach

This technique is not just another way to look at the Big Idea like those above, it uses a different region of the brain to produce it. Books describe freewriting (see Peter Elbow); I formally learned about the technique during my freshman writing seminar at Dartmouth College in 1988. It is a pre-writing technique to generate ideas through rapid association. To succeed at freewriting, you must mentally block out obstacles such as spelling, punctuation, and grammar that normally inhibit the mind from making quick associations.

To use the technique, you write continually without stopping during a predetermined period. As mentioned, you pay no mind to spelling, grammar, legibility (if writing by hand), or even the kids throwing grapes at the cat in the living room. You continue without pause with whatever comes to mind. If nothing comes to mind, you can write about that. While the freeform begins with your object to be interpreted (if you have one), feel free to break away, just follow your line of thought wherever it takes you. The power of freewriting comes in part from putting many ideas before your eyes without barriers and filters that impede what comes next. Having the ideas laid out on the table of your short-term memory allows you to make connections among them and new perspectives of the object. It helps you to explore a new topic, transcend mental barriers (apathy, self-criticism, anxiety, preconceived notions) and generate new mental structures that you hadn't previously considered. When time expires, you read what you wrote and extract that which seems interesting or provocative to you. In a second round, you can freewrite again starting with this seed or nugget discovered in the first. If you feel the nugget is sufficiently provocative you might freewrite about the structure of an argument based on the nugget or move on to your more familiar writing approach to give it structure.

Goldberg provides some rules for freewriting:

- Set a time limit, say five or ten minutes, and then stop

- Keep your hand (or fingers on a keyboard) in constant movement until time elapses. Do not pause, stare off into space, or read what you have written. Write actively.

- Do not pay attention to grammar, spelling, punctuation, neatness, or style. Quality is of no importance, nor correctness. No one else will read this anyway. The goal is to put ideas onto paper or screen.

- If you write astray of your original topic or if you run out of ideas, continue writing nonetheless. If it is necessary to write about senselessness or anything else that passes through your head, do so. You can also write figures similar to words just to keep the hand moving.

- If you feel boredom or discomfort while you write, ask yourself why it bothers you and write about that.

Here's an example of a real freewrite that I did for my other book on heritage interpretation.

> I want a new idea about geology, then I'm thinking about rocks and the effect the effect they have on my idea and I see them every day and almost never think about what they represent and the effect on my liffe. They seems so immovil, what can they tell me? Bu tin reality they are constantly changing since the beginning of the universe. Not immobile. It is simply my view so so so very limited that I can't see how the rocks document millions since birth, on the evolution of the planet. Simply I don't talk the language of rocks and if I could, what stories could they tell me about how rocks come fromouter space, come from the moon and others are cxreated here on Planet Earth. Some even from before the very first organism. If I could speak rock language, my perspective about the universe perhaps would expand to innfinite or at leaset the limits of the universe.

In the discussion of defining a feedback loop, I get the feeling that people may feel that feedback loops are special, to be found occasionally, and are not universally present. Let me make the following proposition, to see if anyone has a counter example: Everything that changes through time is controlled by feedback loops.

Jay Forrester
founder of modern systems dynamics

Contemplation-Meditation Approach

1. Place a meditation cushion or a comfortable chair in a quiet place without disturbances, strong lights, or other stimuli. Lay a notebook and pen next to the cushion.

2. Sit down.

3. Close your eyes and breathe deeply three times.

4. Contemplate the object to be interpreted, reflect on it for as long as it takes.

5. Quickly write down when a potential Big Idea comes into your head.

PEDRO SZEKELY

THEME SPOTLIGHT: A REVELATION-IRONY THEME

Theme: Behind the artistic beauty of the colonial architecture of Antigua, Guatemala, lurks the Conquistadors' hidden plan to dominate indigenous people's own artistic expression and religious customs.

Technique: Successful themes may juxtapose the obvious, outwardly observable or believed by the audience in the first part, with another meaning hidden or revealed in the second.

Pictured above: Antigua Guatemala, World Heritage City, is known as perhaps the best example of colonial architecture in the Americas.

6. Either continue the reflection or move to develop the Big Idea into a theme at your desk.

It is harder to demonstrate an example because this is a process. To write this example, I looked at my computer that helped me to write this *Field Guide*. While I could have written it by hand, indeed, I remember the pre-word processor age in high school, the computer has allowed me to do what I could have otherwise done anyway, but faster and more efficiently. (Let alone saving paper). So, I closed my eyes. I considered how all tools are extensions of human abilities; in a sense, they replace my much more limited body and brain. A calculator replaces my need to do arithmetic. A hammer replaces my need to pound things with my hand or a rock. A car replaces my need to walk and carry things with hands and feet. A computer replaces the need to keep and manipulate multiple elements in my short-term memory. It also allows me to transfer ideas, symbols, and words more quickly to a much more stable medium than my short-term memory.

But what does a robot with advanced artificial intelligence extend and replace? What would be my fate if I was given a Sonny (robot from Asimov's *I, Robot*)? Does it replace my personality, can it eventually replace my soul? Does it extend and replace my longevity and life? What happens when the tool changes from the object to the subject and "we" humans no longer participate in its story?

I open my eyes, type in some notes, and then rewrite my Big Idea into a theme: Technological development has been largely a story of extending and replacing human physical and cognitive capacities to increase productivity, from the simplest functions of hands to perhaps the most advanced functions of the self-reflecting mind.

You notice that I did not include the questions in my theme. My theme is an insight on the universe. I would save the questions to develop my theme in the presentation for the secondary audience. These could be provocative questions if used correctly.

Qualities of Big Ideas
While interpretive themes submit themselves to more defined guidelines, we can still summarize qualities of Big Ideas that should apply most of the time.

One, complete idea
Each Big Idea contains a subject and verb forming a complete sentence and hopefully a single complete idea as well. The exercise of forming a coherent sentence forces clarity on the author.

No: Bird migration to winter feeding grounds

Yes: It is actually more cost effective for birds to migrate thousands of kilometers twice a year than figure out how to survive in winter.

Exciting for the primary audience
As discussed, the primary audience (you) must really like the idea before using it for a secondary audience. If you don't, then, chances are others won't either.

Logical, makes sense
When an idea is not totally clear, lapses in logic can appear. For example, "Although all geological periods to date have been defined based on geological change, our current epoch exhibits a cultural understanding of geology." Do you see it? What does a cultural understanding of geology mean?

Offers a new perspective, revelatory
Big Ideas are not normally just facts. While some facts can be revelatory by themselves, we seek new perspective to our Big Ideas. We seek insight based on facts.

Not revelatory: Sometimes geologic events happen quickly (volcanoes, earthquakes), therefore the new epoch should be renamed the Anthropocene.

Revelatory: Although all geological periods to date have been defined based on geological change, our current epoch shows geologic change occurring on human time scales.

As mentioned, some facts can be new and exciting, reveal new relationships, and illuminate phenomena that cannot easily be verified through relatively simple library or online research. Those facts that we want to avoid are those that are easily verified or already proven or demonstrated (as Ann Lundberg puts it in her article about thesis-based interpretation); they tend simply to generate agreement not provocation. Consider these amazing facts that should be in every interpreter's notebook: "If the rate of expansion one second after the Big Bang had been smaller by even one part in a hundred thousand million million, the universe would have recollapsed before it ever reached its present size," says the late British physicist Stephen Hawking. If you think that is amazing, there are another 35 incredibly improbable reasons that life on earth should not exist and could be evidence that Earth really is special among the gazillions of stars and planets. Search for "Anthropic Principle" and arm yourself with some amazing facts that will truly provoke your audience into thinking about the meaning of human existence.

Be aware, nonetheless, that new perspectives can unsettle people emotionally and also provoke them to disagree with you. This too constitutes provocation which could be seen as meeting the goal of interpretation if it generates thought and audience participation rather than just a knee-jerk emotional reaction. But it also comes with certain risk for you the interpreter as it can expose you to pushback. Part of the art of interpretation is to provoke new or enhanced personal connections without yourself becoming the focus of any discombobulation within the mind of an audience. The goal is for the person or the interpreter to disappear from the connection between audience and heritage. Not being able to disconnect your own ego from the interpretive moment can generate fear which may result in your steering wide of controversial points of view. Ann Lundberg argues that you have to support what you say and shouldn't disturb folks beyond what your evidence and arguments permit. Provocation, as in what an older sibling does to the younger, for its own sake can hurt you and your institution's reputation. As I have mentioned earlier, Lundberg points out that facts easily supported or demonstrated don't have the same likelihood to provoke, since there is little room for debate about them or contribution by the audience. Several examples of related truths follow that are both easily supported and demonstrated and also not easily supported and demonstrated. Can you feel the difference in provocation power?

Clear, but not necessarily quickly understood
Some ideas challenge even when written clearly; they take time to process. Sometimes Big Ideas can also leave readers with more questions than answers. It might also be considered that in this Information Age, when answers are easily obtained, it is this provocation for questions that reflects an interpreter's true value. A strong vehicle could increase clarity and processing, but a complex idea may still be a complex idea. Consider these examples, all vetted through time.

- "The probability of a shift in worldview is directly proportional to the extent we acknowledge that we are not dealing with isolated trends." —Mark Woodhouse

- "Reality divided by reason always leaves a remainder." —Daniel Kim

- After the Big Bang, every distinction is arbitrary. —Buckminster Fuller (Allegedly)

- "To optimize the whole, we must sub-optimize the parts." —W. Edward Deming

- "We can see how every truth and every error, each a thought of someone's mind, clothes itself with societies, houses, cities, language, ceremonies, newspapers." —Ralph Waldo Emerson

Easily Supported and Demonstrated	Not Easily Supported and Demonstrated	Possible Supporting Evidence
The entire universe as we know it flared forth from an infinitesimally small point nearly 15 billion years ago.	Humans can access the ground of being, that intangible field out of which tangible material arises now, before the Big Bang, and possibly forever.	From the moment of the Big Bang forward, scientists can measure ancient background microwave radiation and calculate the rate of the universe's expansion outward from that original point. The red shift is another technique for measuring time across space. Before the Big Bang, empirical science had little if anything to say. Spiritual teachers, meditators, and metaphysical philosophers, on the other hand, argue that a field of infinite potential exists and has always existed and is accessible through deep meditation. The evidence then is direct experience of this field; many millions of people throughout history have experienced it, written about it, and teach how to access it.
The once traditional practice of acupuncture can relieve a variety of gastrointestinal ills.	The traditional practice of arm rubbing can relieve many digestive ills.	Both acupuncture and Central American arm rubbing are varieties of reflexology, the application of pressure to specific points that correspond to bodily organs and functions. Formal scientific studies support the effects of acupuncture, while arm rubbing relies more on the anecdotes of many people across time and place.
People's existence transcends the time marked by birth and death through memory of their personal legacies.	People may be literally connected to each other beyond the boundaries of birth and death.	The first theme is easily proven; all of history is based on remembering what people have done. The second may refer to aspects of existence beyond historical documentation, for example, reincarnation. Dr. Jim Tucker at the University of Virginia has been studying past-life memories from children and has created a large, rigorous dataset.
A great flood punished the Mediterranean region, shaping today's regional landscape.	God sent the Great Flood to punish infidelity.	Geologists have theorized that the Zanclean flood filled a dry Mediterranean basin more than 5 million years ago, based in part on erosion features taken from sediment data. The second is supported by Biblical text, faith-based worldview, and perhaps direct divine testimony after death.

Universal

If a Big Idea is truly big then it should illuminate truths greater than just our own site or whatever object we happen to interpret. These truths should ring relevant and provocative for the primary and at least some secondary audiences. If we avoid any mention of our local site or object, then we can more easily resist the temptation to simply describe the local site and rather focus on the bigger picture. It is very helpful to assume this stance with respect to your site and your Big Idea: "My site is a great example of this Big Idea; it is a great place to interpret it." So, in effect, if you have written a local idea or theme that talks directly about your site (which is an okay place to start on your quest toward a Big Idea and later a strong interpretive theme), consider universalizing that idea to make it more relevant to more people. In any event, if you interpret the theme at your site, people will quickly understand that your site has something to do with the presentation, even if you don't declare it immediately.

The table on the following page converts local ideas into Big Ideas with universal relevance. The themes on the left come from published interpretive plans, available on the internet at the time of this writing. Please note while these examples are themes, it is far better to ensure universal relevance when you develop your Big Idea than wait until you wordsmith a final interpretive theme.

After you have written the Big Idea and theme with universal relevance, if you like, you can add your site as an example, which can increase approval by local stakeholders and increase local relevance even further. Consider these themes with a Big Idea and local reference.

- Fifteenth- and sixteenth-century military coastal forts like Fort Jesus in Mombasa, Kenya, protected, consolidated, and coordinated East African trade and sea routes to the Far East for the dominant foreign powers, hence the control of what would have otherwise remained in the chaos of piracy and conflict.

- There is no such thing as natural disasters, only natural phenomena, such as Hurricanes Harvey, Michael, and María, which damage human systems built with development decisions that do not prioritize resilience.

Do beware, nonetheless, that universal should not be confused with overly general. A strong interpretive theme reveals a universal truth that helps to explain the human condition in a new or enhanced way. People can also write something so general and generic that it applies to everything but does not reveal anything. Lisa Brochu decries what she calls the fill-in-the-blank theme: themes that are true virtually anywhere and therefore irrelevant. Usually such themes contain

Local Theme	Universalized Theme	Observations
The Life and Times of a Patriot As a signer of the Declaration of Independence, William Floyd, prominent New York political leader and wealthy plantation owner, provides a personal perspective on the risks to life, property, and reputation associated with being a patriot in New York during the War for Independence.	As governments or ways of governing change, often it is necessary to destroy the previous form and sometimes those who promote the change as well.	William Floyd is a great, local example of a class of American revolutionaries who themselves represent a larger reality seen throughout the world and history. But with the universalized theme we don't confuse the focus by spending too much time on the details of one man and not enough on the larger, more consequential truth.
The Grand Prairie experiences damage to and renewal of its ecosystems throughout time.	All ecosystems eventually experience some natural "disaster" or violent change (forest fires, earthquakes, hurricanes) that rapidly releases their energy (for example, stored as trees) which then is reused in a new phase of growth and evolution.	The Grand Prairie does not experience anything unique in this sense; in fact, all ecosystems pass through a cycle of buildup and release of energy. This includes human ecosystems such as civilizations. This underlying pattern is far more meaningful than to describe the Grand Prairie's experience anecdotally and without reference to larger universal processes.
Captain John Smith's voyages on the Chesapeake, and his subsequent maps and writings, profoundly impacted world politics and the evolution of our nation by spurring European settlement of the Bay region and the eastern seaboard, influencing colonial affairs for more than a century, disrupting the native peoples' lifeways in the mid-Atlantic, and increasing human influences on the Bay environment.	Colonization of new lands speeds up as the colonizers learn more about those new lands. *Could mention Captain Smith in this universalized theme for local purposes, without hurting the universally relevant theme:* Colonization of new lands speeds up as the colonizers learn more about those new lands, such as through the writings and adventures of Captain John Smith.	This wordy and largely fact-based statement points to universal significance ("profoundly impacted world politics and the evolution of our nation") without clearly stating an insight or Big Idea. Nonetheless, John Smith is a great example of numerous potential themes. As the second example shows, it is okay to mention a local heritage element once the Big Idea is clearly articulated.
Necessity and Innovation: Life in Alaska requires adaptability and ingenuity, qualities that can frequently be seen in the ways Alaskans have invented and modified technologies. (Extremes, Innovation, Survival)	Because human ability to adapt is based on our innovative technological mind rather than our physical bodies, our species has colonized almost all habitats on planet Earth. Or The evolution of cultural memes rather than biological genes has allowed humans to rapidly adapt to nearly all habitats on planet Earth.	Adaptability and ingenuity are nothing specific to Alaskans and to a certain extent not specific to humans either. Nonetheless Alaskans and the perceived hostility and difficulty in living in the far north can make an excellent story of this much broader truth about adaptation.

unprovocative generalized facts. "XYZ site is a kaleidoscope of natural and cultural history that is managed for the enjoyment of the people." We won't even mention its kaleidoscopic ambiguity.

Station 4 Big Ideas

1. Big Ideas have the power to provoke, inspire, and even transform people. They are, nonetheless, audience-dependent.

> The major problems in the world are the result of the difference between the way nature works and the way people think.
>
> *Gregory Bateson*

2. Researching a topic allows the researcher to encounter new ideas and perspectives about the interpreted object, increasing the likelihood of either discovering or developing a Big Idea about it.

3. There are multiple techniques to ignite inspiration in the act of developing the Big Idea.

4. Facts can provoke audience thought, especially when those facts are not easily supported or demonstrated.

5. Several qualities characterize most Big Ideas.

6. It is good practice to omit mention of a particular site in order to focus on the universal value of the Big Idea. The site can later be added merely as an example, useful for local relevance.

7. Audience disagreement with a Big Idea is consistent with the objectives of interpretation when that disagreement is accompanied by thinking and audience participation rather than just a knee-jerk emotional rejection to the idea.

8. An interpreter defends him or herself against pushback, and the fear of receiving pushback, by having prepared the evidence and arguments necessary to support the presented Big Idea.

STATION 4 EXERCISE

Answers to station exercises can be found in the Field Notes starting on page 115.

Big Idea Test

Check each criterion that applies to each proposed Big Idea; you may put a question mark when it is not possible to determine. This test presupposes that the statement has already been determined to be an interpretive statement.

Big Idea	Complete	Exciting	Logical	Revelatory	Clear	Universal
People believe their creation myths to help them understand their place in the world.						
Human-produced greenhouse gases speed up climate change way beyond our ability to adapt to it.						
Iguazu National Park is a World Heritage bi-national park.						
Popular super heroes symbolize human psychological archetypes.						
Democracy is more a measure of social capital.						
"The universe is made of stories, not atoms." —Muriel Rukeyser						
"The most important scientific revolutions all include, as their only common feature, the dethronement of human arrogance from one pedestal after another of previous convictions about our centrality in the cosmos." —Stephen Jay Gould						

Theme Notes

The Big Idea Develops within the Audience's Mind via a Vehicle

A Big Idea without a vehicle (see Station 3) may be at worst an inarticulate notion or at best a great idea that few people read; a vehicle without a Big Idea is at best fancy writing, gimmickry, or just boring. They need each other. You need them both. The vehicle then represents the theme sentence(s) that places the Big Idea before the audience for its consideration. It proposes the Big Idea for development by both primary and secondary audiences. It can do this directly if read or recited but most of the time it occurs through an intermediary, the interpreter and his or her presentation. It gives specific direction to the interpreter who develops personal and non-personal media.

One frequent problem for those who confuse the two results is what I call postponing the Big Idea." That is, you write a theme statement, a vehicle, without clearly including the Big Idea. If theme writers are aware of the need for a Big Idea, they may be postponing it because they don't want to spend the time to ignite their inspiration. Otherwise the theme writer suffers a deeper misunderstanding about interpretation

A book isn't a single, static thing with one unarguable meaning. Each reader who comes to it brings his own special knowledge, habits, and attitudes. Each reader reads a different book. Each reader imagines a different story. A few years ago, for instance, a friend of my mother's sent me a copy of a test on [my book] *Rite of Passage* that she had given her students. The first question read: "True or False? The theme of *Rite of Passage* is…" I can't tell you what the presumed theme was, but I can tell you that I didn't recognize it. Beads of sweat leaped out of my forehead. After two more questions, I had to put the test aside. I didn't know the 'right' answers.

Alexei Panshin

itself, confusing it with information or education. Among the traps that result in postponing the Big Idea include the following:

1. Hiding behind an adjective like "important" or "special": "Despite their just standing there, trees actually communicate with each other through very important mechanisms." So, what are the mechanisms?

2. Using clever wording instead of a Big Idea: "To many a lost landscape, to others Lake Pope represents a landscape of hope." Sounds good, but where's the beef?

3. Writing it like a mystery that the visitor will discover. Mystery can tantalize the audience during a thematic presentation; but it usually does not help a theme, because it withholds crucial information indicating that the writer may not have a Big Idea at all: "While the conquest brought fortune to the Spanish and misfortune to the Native Americans, it also brought something very special for generations to come." The whole point of this theme revolves around what the conquest brought for future generations. So why not state it? If not now, when?

4. Labeling the new idea without mentioning what it is: "This time period marks the emergence of a new form of tourism." Another: "Despite millions of years of Earth history based on geological change, there might be a need for a new way to name it."

5. Asking questions instead of offering insight: "Might this next geologic stage named for humankind also bring an end to it?"

6. Using vague language: "The historic trail created connections between people and places in many ways." Or: "To protect the panda is to restore the balance between people and nature."

If the Big Idea doesn't ring clearly at the time of writing the theme, it will not likely emerge later. We must differentiate therefore between the Big Idea and the vehicle, especially for those who have not yet mastered the craft. For experienced theme writers, they intuitively write their themes endowed with Big Ideas and a vehicle from the start.

Provocative Themes Are Relevant and Motivate People to Think about Them

To reiterate, theme strength derives from provocation likelihood and ease of processing. Sam presents the scientific background for these components in his book. Suffice to say that provocation refers to the likelihood that the audience will think about the theme or the thematic presentation. The more relevant the audience regards the Big Idea, the more and longer they will think about it, forming more connections and deepening their relationship with it. Likewise, the easier the theme is to process mentally for the audience, the more likely they will think about it (remembering that the final theme or vehicle may have elements such as examples, readable text, and well-chosen metaphors to make the Big Idea more provocative and easier to process). We have already seen some provocative elements for Big Ideas; below I'll show you a few more as well as ways to make a theme easier to understand and process.

> When you begin with a strong, thought-provoking theme, you're already close to success.
>
> *Sam Ham*

1. Connect to the audience's background, experience, and expectations to make it more personal and relevant. You can do these by referring to concepts and examples familiar to the audience.

2. Use the audience's language or words and expressions for themes that will be shared directly with them.

3. Apply Knockan Theory. Sam explains the theory in his book (Chapter 7) which you can see in the figure from the Interpretive Theme Writer's Worksheet in the Field Notes. Basically, it identifies several parameters that, for psychological and perhaps evolutionary reasons, attract people's attention. Find these parameters hidden in your theme and make them explicit. These variables (surely not an exhaustive list) include humanity, life, sex, surprise, novelty, age, size, and movement. Without a Big Idea a writer may use these as simple attention-grabbers or gimmicks, but with a Big Idea, they can accentuate important features and increase provocation. See the examples in the table on the next page.

4. Add in other spicy ingredients. Most writers regularly mix these ingredients into their writing and should become common residents on the theme writer's pantry shelf if not already.
    -   Suspense, mystery: "The invention of printing radically changed ways of thinking—not just how things are communicated, but what can be thought."—Derrick de Kerckhove. Don't you want to know what can be thought or how thought changed? Granted, this is a theme likely shown to the public given the mystery; if the theme is implicit, you have little justification to include mystery. The author better know what changed in what can be thought in order to use this ingredient and not just postpone the Big Idea with it.

Parameter	Less interesting	More interesting
Age	All of Earth's history is divided into geological time periods until the present; now scientists may rename the current epoch as the Anthropocene after mere millennia of human alteration.	Four and a half billion years of Earth's deep time have produced all the geological time periods until present; now scientists may rename the current epoch as the Anthropocene after mere millennia of human alteration.
Life	Earth's geological time periods changed because of geological change, while human building and cropping for mere thousands of years may result in the naming of the Anthropocene Epoch.	Two hundred million years of dinosaurian dominance on Earth did not influence naming of geological time periods, while human building and cropping for mere thousands may result in the naming of the Anthropocene Epoch.
Movement and Size	Until now the name of Earth's time periods relied only on geological change over time; the next period however may be named solely for human civilization-building.	Until now the naming of Earth's geological time periods has relied exclusively on colossal churning, mixing, and solidifying of megatons of rocks over eons; the next period however may be named solely for human civilization-building.

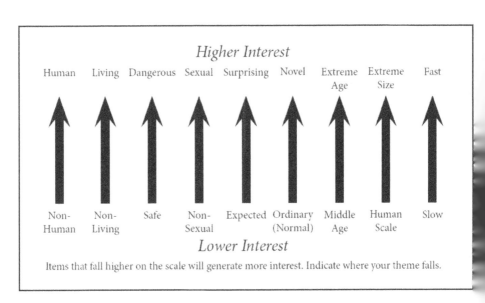

Higher Interest

Human	Living	Dangerous	Sexual	Surprising	Novel	Extreme Age	Extreme Size	Fast
Non-Human	Non-Living	Safe	Non-Sexual	Expected	Ordinary (Normal)	Middle Age	Human Scale	Slow

Lower Interest

Items that fall higher on the scale will generate more interest. Indicate where your theme falls.

- Tension: Here I offer two examples both similar and famous. They directly talk about the conflict and challenge that promoters of new ideas face in their quest to implement those ideas.
  - ~ "[T]here is nothing more difficult to carry out, nor more doubtful of success, nor more dangerous to handle, than to initiate a new order of things. For the reformer has enemies in all those who profit by the old order, and only lukewarm defenders in all those who would profit by the new order." —Niccolò Machiavelli.

    > If a theme or idea is too near the surface, the novel becomes simply a tract illustrating an idea.
    > *Elizabeth Bowen*

  - ~ "Almost always the men who achieve these fundamental inventions of a new paradigm have been either very young or very new to the field whose paradigm they change." —Thomas Kuhn.
- Irony: Two examples from the interpretive framework of El Cocuy National Park in Colombia:
  - ~ "Throwing Salt on the Sacred Wound: Commerce along the Salt Route unleashed a wave of desecration of indigenous territory." The irony is that the Spanish conquerors took the indigenous trade routes used to promote prosperity and used these routes against their creators.
  - ~ Now one of this theme's sub-themes: "Despite the fact that the Spanish brought the Holy Cross to extend their religion over the indigenous cosmovision, in reality, they desecrated their land."
  - ~ A theme from Fort Jesus National Monument in Kenya: "Fifteenth- and sixteenth-century global economic powers, like Portugal, Spain, and Oman battled to dominate the lifeblood trade routes of the high seas, yet their oceanic success depended ironically on land-bound forts."
  - ~ Another from Fort Jesus: "Mombasa's strategic location, critical for controlling the East African trade routes, attracted fierce competitors from distant Europe and Asia. Yet the violent and on-going clashes which led to Fort Jesus changing hands six times, ironically seeded a diverse and tolerant cultural mix of peoples living there today." It is not necessary to include "ironically" but it makes the technique clearer for demonstration purposes.
- Paradox: "The only thing that I know, is that I know nothing." —DesCartes. You could argue this is not an interpretive theme because it uses first person; it is a deep philosophical theme statement nevertheless that has been debated across books and centuries.

- Confront myths: "Many biologists believe that evolution refers only to biology, but, in reality, evolution goes much beyond Darwin, beginning with the Big Bang." This can be similar to the irony revelation technique where the theme contains both the common belief or myth and reveals a new idea or perspective to modify or overthrow it.
- Capture complexity, dynamics (universal processes).
  ~ An example from the Flint Hills Discovery Center interpretive framework in Kansas: "In recent centuries, the Flint Hills have suffered various displacements of its (non)human inhabitants, leaving behind fragmented communities, but enriching its overall natural and cultural diversity." To understand complexity and universal processes, though it may take more effort, often provides a greater richness of understanding about how things work.
  ~ From the Valle de Oro National Wildlife Refuge interpretive framework: "Migration and cultivation, traditionally guided by natural cycles, have been fragmented by modern transportation and production systems creating complex landscape mosaics."
- Influences over great time and distance (without sacrificing clarity of the Big Idea): "Governments fight drug trafficking in Colombia where local farmers grow coca, while invisible and blameless consumers in distant lands drive demand for cocaine."
- Alliteration, rhythm, repetition, and other wording techniques:
  ~ "As far as the laws of mathematics refer to reality, they are not certain; and as far as they are certain, they do not refer to reality." —Albert Einstein
  ~ "What distinguishes World Heritage Sites from other protected areas is the ease with which the Sites can tie together the heart of a person with the heart of humanity."

5. Subject appropriateness. A theme's subject should relate to the interpreted object (such as the heritage). Themes almost never should talk about visitors, interpretive medium, activity, probably not about tourism, or heritage managers. If you mention any of these, you probably don't have an interpretive theme; you may have an objective or just a fact. I did once write a theme about trails for people who studied trails. In that case, trails really were the object of interpretation.

Left: Mother Teresa's house-turned-museum in Skopje, Macedonia
Right: Museum interpreter at Mother Teresa's house

THEME SPOTLIGHT: TRANSFORMATIVE THEMES TAP DEEP TRUTHS

Theme: Raised with unconditional love in Skopje, Mother Theresa demonstrated that while the body must have food, water, air, and shelter to survive, only unconditional love can heal damages to the spirit, open doors closed by hate, and restore even the most indigent to dignity.

Technique: Interpretation at its most powerful very much resembles spiritual growth or even the goal of enlightenment; both integrate your awareness into the fundamental nature of the universe. Thus, the more interpretation can dive from leaves to roots, the greater its transformational power. Akin to interpreters, spiritual teachers and gurus also create opportunities for their students to taste the nature of ultimate or universal truths.

Are the mystics and sages insane? Because they all tell variations on the same story, don't they? The story of awakening one morning and discovering you are one with the All, in a timeless and eternal and infinite fashion. Yes, maybe they are crazy, these divine fools... Maybe the evolutionary sequence really is from matter to body to mind to soul to spirit, each transcending and including, each with a greater depth and greater consciousness and wider embrace. And in the highest reaches of evolution, maybe, just maybe, an individual's consciousness does indeed touch infinity—a total embrace of the entire Kosmos—a Kosmic consciousness that is Spirit awakened to its own true nature. It's at least plausible." —Ken Wilber

THEME SPOTLIGHT: ADDING HUMANITY TO NON-HUMAN PHENOMENA

Theme: Ants innovated farming strategies (aphid herding and fungi cultivation) millennia before people "invented" their own farming systems.

Technique: Even purely natural science ideas can relate to the human condition to make the Big Idea more relevant to people and thus more impactful. Look for where ecological and evolutionary processes, adaptations, and behaviors overlap between humans and other organisms. Seen this way, humans experience many of the same processes, limitations, and realities with other organisms, even bacteria. Can you think of them?

Pictured above: Leafcutter ants haul this petal back to their nest where they will feed it to fungi which in turn the ants harvest and eat in an utterly formic subsistence economy.

Provocative Themes Are Easy to Process

As mentioned above, theme provocation depends on relevance and processing ease. The following techniques can make a theme easier on the eyes and on the mind, liberating brainpower to think about the theme's implications rather than think about what the theme writer wants to say.

1. Brevity. In *Environmental Interpretation*, Sam advocated the one-sentence rule for themes. Although he no longer abides strictly by that restriction in all cases (see Ham 2013, p. 127–128, 145), he still values the spirit behind the rule: Include just enough relevant detail so that people understand the idea and are motivated to think about it without being given any additional background. If you can accomplish this in one thought-provoking sentence, great. But if you need two (or rarely three) related sentences, that's okay too as long as they together capture a single relevant idea in a thought-provoking way.

> All stories interest me, and some haunt me until I end up writing them. Certain themes keep coming up: justice, loyalty, violence, death, political and social issues, freedom.
>
> *Isabel Allende*

   - Short theme: "The health of a democratic society may be measured by the quality of functions performed by private citizens." —Alexis de Tocqueville
   - Long theme: "Our culture does not nourish that which is best or noblest in the human spirit. It does not cultivate vision, imagination, or aesthetic or spiritual sensitivity. It does not encourage gentleness, generosity, caring, or compassion. Increasingly in the late 20th Century, the economic-technocratic-statist worldview has become a monstrous destroyer of what is loving and life-affirming in the human soul."—Ron Miller

2. Word economy. While brevity refers to word quantity, economy refers to word quality. Economy breeds readability, while wordiness unleashes boredom. Readability is a measurable quality of a sentence, paragraph, or entire book. It combines three variables: number of words, sentence length, and word length.
   - Lower readability: "The naming of Earth's geological time periods has relied exclusively on the colossal churning, mixing, and solidifying of megatons of rocks during eons until now, when the next time period may be named solely for human civilization-building."
   - Greater readability: "To date, Earth's geologic time periods have been named only for changing rocks. Now, the current period may be renamed for human activity."

THEME SPOTLIGHT: CAN A THEME HAVE MORE THAN ONE SENTENCE?

Theme: "For just as the Milky Way is the universe in the form of a flower, we are the universe in the form of a human. And every time we are drawn to look up in the night sky and reflect on the awesome beauty of the universe, we are actually the universe reflecting on itself." —Brian Swimme

Technique: The one- or two-sentence "rule" was to obligate interpreters to get quickly to the point without distracting text. Good writing, however, enjoys the luxury of a few sentences if each sentence contributes to a clear, provocative Big Idea. In this example, the theme statement is basically a mini-argument, told quickly yet elegantly.

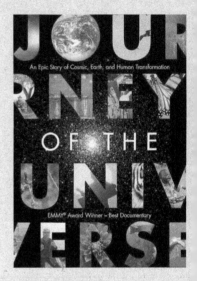

We measured the readability of these two themes at www.read-able.com (there are other similar sites) simply by cutting and pasting the text into the reader. You can see the results in the figures on the next page. Which results correspond to which theme?

3. Figurative language (simile, metaphor, exaggeration, personification, etc.) and examples. Through comparison and example, you can make ideas easier to understand. Generally, the clearer the writing, the less need exists for figurative language (see different kinds of figures at https://literarydevices.net/figurative-language), examples, adjectives, and adverbs. Doctor's warning: Do not use when they reduce clarity. This item may seem to contradict earlier advice on avoiding metaphors, but the difference turns on whether the metaphor amplifies meaning or hides it.

    *   Example of an example: "Although all geological periods to date have been defined based on geological change, our current epoch exhibits geologic change—such as Glacier National Park's melting glaciers—in human time."
    *   Metaphor: "By applying a remedy to one sore, you will provoke another: and that which removes the one ill symptom produces others, whereas the strengthening one part of the body weakens the rest." —Sir Thomas More, *Utopia.*

READABILITY INDICES

Flesh Kincaid Reading Ease	14.6
Flesh Kincaid Grade Level	20.7
Gunning Fog Score	23.6
SMOG Index	16.3
Coleman Liau Index	15
Automated Readability Index	22.2

TEXT STATISTICS

No. of sentences	1
No. of words	38
No. of complex words	8
Percent of complex words	21.05%
Average words per sentence	38.00
Average syllables per word	1.82

READABILITY INDICES

Flesh Kincaid Reading Ease	54.9
Flesh Kincaid Grade Level	7.8
Gunning Fog Score	11.2
SMOG Index	7.6
Coleman Liau Index	13.6
Automated Readability Index	6.5

TEXT STATISTICS

No. of sentences	3
No. of words	26
No. of complex words	5
Percent of complex words	19.23%
Average words per sentence	8.67
Average syllables per word	1.69

- Personification: "As the geology field gazed upon acts of humanity, it knew that it could no longer name its time periods for geological criteria alone."
- Metonymy (where a closely related thing represents the thing): "Crowns throughout history always fight to retain their power even when the weary people demand a change."
- Imagery: "The maritime discoverers sailed their cultural and urban models around the world."
- Synecdoche (where a part represents the whole): "The eyes see only what the mind is prepared to comprehend." —Henri Bergson.
- Irony: "Bullies are often people who are shy and can't make friends easily, so, as the theme of the movie 'A Bronx Tale' tells us, it is better to be feared if you can't be loved." —Philip Zimbardo

4. You/we/us. Sometimes when you use "you," the reader can take offense, declaring that this theme doesn't apply to them or how dare you, the theme writer, think you know him or her, the reader. So generally, avoid such use. As almost always, the reaction does depend on the audience and the intended Zone of Tolerance (Chapter 8). For example, "Our misunderstanding of climate change has delayed

THEME SPOTLIGHT: POETRY IS GREAT FOR PROVOCATION, BAD FOR THEME CLARITY

Poem:

Two roads diverged in a yellow wood,
And sorry I could not travel both
And be one traveler, long I stood
And looked down one as far as I could
To where it bent in the undergrowth;

Then took the other, as just as fair,
And having perhaps the better claim,
Because it was grassy and wanted wear;
Though as for that the passing there
Had worn them really about the same,

And both that morning equally lay
In leaves no step had trodden black.
Oh, I kept the first for another day!
Yet knowing how way leads on to way,
I doubted if I should ever come back.

I shall be telling this with a sigh
Somewhere ages and ages hence:
Two roads diverged in a wood, and I—
I took the one less traveled by,
And that has made all the difference.

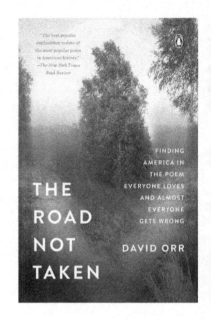

"The best popular explanation to date of the most popular poem in American history."
—*The New York Times Book Review*

FINDING
AMERICA IN
THE POEM
EVERYONE LOVES
AND ALMOST
EVERYONE
GETS WRONG

THE
ROAD
NOT
TAKEN

DAVID ORR

Technique:

Poetry can be marvelously provocative and highly effective during a thematic presentation; but if poetry is in the theme itself, not even the staff may know or share a single understanding of what the theme wants to say. Here, Frost wrote one of America's most famous poems whose interpretation is both wide-ranging and, according to one English professor, generally wrong.

its remediation."—"Hey, I didn't misunderstand it!" You can insert "you" into a theme if it truly represents everyone in a generic sense. In fiction, where the theme is implicit, it hardly matters, although one line from a character (remember DesCartes's famous line above) could encapsulate the theme. Here are two examples of generic yous.

- "The one recurring theme in my writing, and in my life in general, is confusion. The fact that anytime you think you really know something, you're going to find out you're wrong—that is the rule. The moments where you think you have something figured out, those are the exceptions." —Conor Oberst

- "You can never change things by fighting the existing reality. To change something, build a new model that makes the existing model obsolete." —F. Buckminster Fuller

> I teach some film criticism courses around Boston, and I tell students there are empty-calorie words such as "amazing" and "awesome." These don't really convey any actual meaning other than bigness. When I first started at *The Boston Globe* somebody said, "Don't ever use the word 'compelling.' Whenever a movie is called compelling, I know it's going to bore me."
>
> *Ty Burr*

5. Prohibited words (subjective adjectives). We commonly use adjectives when we don't know how more concretely or precisely to describe things. An entire class of subjective adjectives — important, special, marvelous, amazing, outstanding, incredible, significant, magnificent—furthermore convey no specific meanings and cannot conjure images in your mind. They only point to a general feeling. Worse, they can hide meanings that our themes should make explicit. For example, "Our planet is an important paradise named geologically for its changing rocks." Why is that "important"?

> If there were only one truth, you couldn't paint a hundred canvases on the same theme.
>
> *Pablo Picasso*

6. Clichés and unclear figurative language. Similar to "prohibited" adjectives, a variety of clichés and metaphors can also hide the real meaning of a theme. Thus, in general avoid words like *treasure, jewel, gem, marvels, paradise, heaven*, and noun forms of subjective adjectives such as *importance, significance,*

amazement, and so on. Below are three themes that due to the use of metaphor are not clear without significantly more context or explanation.

- "Yellowstone is an American jewel, marvelous for studying rock layers that help name geological time periods."
- "The theme is the theme of humiliation, which is the square root of sin, as opposed to the freedom from humiliation, and love, which is the square root of wonderful." —Carson McCullers
- "The voyage of the best ship is a zigzag line of a hundred tacks." —Ralph Waldo Emerson

7. Clarity over poetry. Poetry is a powerful form of written expression precisely because it provokes you to think and interpret. But that provocation may come from the Big Idea, or it may come from intentional ambiguity that can be interpreted in multiple ways. Consider the poem in the margin by William Blake. For a theme, however, we need ultimate clarity so that the entire team understands the meaning and plans accordingly and consistently. But remember the powerful role poetry can play when presenting your primary theme to a secondary audience.

> Both read the *Bible* day and night, But thou read black, where I read white.
> *William Blake*

- Poetry: "Our forest cathedral sings gospel in its majesty and truth in its longevity."
- Clarity: "Because primary forests bear few if any recognizable signs of humanity, people associate them with prehistory, a time once considered purer and closer to the divine."

8. Strong verbs and nouns. Strong verbs and nouns through their specificity project images in the audience's mind, thus intensifying the experience. Consider the best strategy, therefore, to avoid the use of adjectives, the verb "to be" which produces no mental image whatsoever, and gerunds (verbs with an –ing such as running). Writing teachers often say that writers supplement with adjectives when their nouns suffer weakness and bolster with adverbs when their verbs lack power. Look in the Field Notes for Sam's list of strong action verbs.

- Weak: Humans have made many big changes to the planet's natural surface, an especially important motive to change the name to the Anthropocene.
- Strong: From sea-bottom sediments to molecules that bounce in the sky, humans have scarred the entire planet surface, provoking the arrival of the Anthropocene.

9. Active voice. Similar to the previous point, but worthy of its own spot on this list, passive voice hides the subject of the action which clouds mental imagery. If you cannot see the actor, your mind picture remains incomplete and far less intense.
   - Passive: Until now, time periods have been named for changes in geology; now it is proposed to rename the current epoch based on anthropology.
   - Active: Until now, scientists have named time periods based on changes in geology; now, they propose to rename the current epoch based on anthropology.

> Every adjective and adverb is worth five cents. Every verb is worth fifty cents.
>
> *Mary Oliver*

10. Specificity. Following above, specificity paints images in the mind while vagueness and generality muck it up, greatly injuring the experience and processing ease. For this reason, also avoid such phrases as "represents," "is a symbol of," or "symbolizes." Just specify what it symbolizes without labeling it.
    - Vague: This site symbolizes natural patterns.
    - Specific: Eight sacred symbols, such as the triskelion and the sun, recur in rock formations that dot the landscape.

While on specificity, many people confuse generality (how specific are examples and points) with universality (scale: local, regional, global, universal). The following table distinguishes between the two measures.

Different Scales	General	Specific
Universal	Though today we commonly associate globalization with virtual economic entities, globalization was born arguably with ancient maritime explorers.	Though today we commonly associate globalization with virtual entities such as the Internet and worldwide banking, when globalization was born, arguably with the Portuguese Discoverers in the 15th Century, physical military fortifications such as Fort Jesus tied together their globalizing threads.
Local	Those who followed the initial explorers set up forts to defend shipping lanes around Africa.	Fort Jesus in Mombasa defended Portuguese shipping lanes before the advent of canons rendered the fort obsolete.

11. Power positions. According to communication theory, the beginning and ending of a sentence (or paragraph or entire story) wield the greatest power. The beginning because people pay a lot of attention and the end because they remember best the last thing they see and hear. If you can deploy key words in power positions, they can leave a stronger impression. "Earth's history has always earned its time-period names based on geological change; now, for the first time, scientists propose renaming the current epoch for human change."

> Art is built on the deepest themes of human meaning: good and evil, beauty and ugliness, life and death, love and hate. No other story has incarnated those themes more than the story of Jesus.
>
> *John Ortberg*

Your Theme Should Pass the Strong Theme Test

Once you have written and rewritten at least two theme drafts, apply this test and see how you do. If you answer "yes" to every question, good chance you're on the trail toward a strong theme.

1. Is the theme interpretive rather than some other statement?

2. Does it provoke rather than just provide easily verifiable information?

3. Does it avoid postponing the Big Idea?

4. Does it excite you? Do you want to know more?

5. Can you imagine an entire program based on this theme?

Station 5 Big Ideas

1. Theme strength depends on provocation likelihood (which depends both on audience relevance and processing ease).

2. A variety of techniques improve both relevance and processing ease.

3. Interpreters often confuse generality and universality. The first refers to the number of details about something while the second refers to the scale at which the statement applies or is true.

STATION 5 EXERCISES

Answers to station exercises can be found in the Field Notes starting on page 115.

1. Weak vs. Strong Theme Practice

Theme	Strong or Weak	Why?
Since even small isolated plots of Lower Rio Grande Valley chaparral serve birds in the migratory flyway, habitat defragmentation can begin with backyards, unlike traditional conservation that begins with large blocks of habitat.		
Adios to the heritage		
The World Birding Center sites are portals to the rich birding matrix of the Lower Rio Grande Valley.		
Conservationists and ranchers both share a love for the same land in south Texas; their traditional mutual animosity is a leftover from 20th-century thinking.		
The Pueblo Culture Center traces the culture of the Pueblo Peoples.		
The diversity and contrast of landscapes around the Middle Rio Grande Valley make it an interesting place.		
Hot summer days in Madrid		
The destruction began here at Jamestown.		
Protect the wildlife of Ashton Lagoon!		
Draining the lagoon of its water damages the ecosystem.		
Though hardening of the Rio Grande river channel has ended natural periodic flooding of riparian habitats, humans have inadvertently recreated this natural function with its acequia system.		
The autonomous power of traditional wildlife refuge managers has empowered the public around Valle de Oro National Wildlife Refuge to participate in its management.		
Artificial wetlands in Lower Rio Grande Valley eventually become real wetlands when water flow is restored from the Rio Grande.		
Birds and butterflies both fly through the Greek islands.		
The Caribbean is a major byway not just for birds, but for people as well.		
The PUP Global Heritage Consortium has many interesting partners.		
Different people with different perspectives interpret the same events through completely different eyes, such as Hurricane Harvey, which could be God's punishment, a random event, or an effect of increasing Climate Chaos.		

2. Fill in the table with yes or no or an argument why you cannot definitively answer either way.

Questions/Themes	Since a single evolutionary force creates all heritage, the only difference between natural and cultural heritage are university departments that study them.	God is the universal force that drives all evolution of heritage.	Every culture in history has had a static worldview after world creation until modern science.
Is the theme interpretive rather than some other statement?			
Does it provoke rather than just provide easily verifiable information?			
Does it avoid postponing the Big Idea?			
Does it excite you? Do you want to know more?			
Can you imagine an entire program based on this theme?			
Does it pass the test?			

Theme Notes

Theme Writing Can be Individual-, Team-, or Community-Based

Virtually all interpretive texts that mention theme writing, even in passing, assume the perspective of the single theme writer behind a desk. Yet, in reality, not just individuals write themes but teams and even communities do as well. For this reason, at this station we talk about how themes emerge at these different scales and how you can improve that creative process.

Sometimes the scale at which themes take shape is obvious. You are an interpreter and need a theme for tomorrow's program. Get to it. Other times a creative team develops an exhibition, and together they must come up with the overarching theme. Rarer still, a park might see interpretation as a community process that increases local people's ownership of the heritage and tourism, so they involve community members in identifying the Big Ideas most important to them. So, the level at which people craft themes depends on the conditions and needs. Some questions that influence that decision:

- Whose meanings or ideas about heritage are most important?

- Who is the primary/secondary audience?

- What are the objectives? Whose Zone of Tolerance prevails (individual, team, or community)?

- How much time does the heritage site have to prepare?

- Who needs to be involved to produce the medium?

- Are there resources to facilitate a community-based process?

THEME SPOTLIGHT: ALL THREE LEVELS CAN INTERACT

Theme:

"Safe Distance: Although Western culture impacted the heritage of many indigenous people, the Emberá have conserved their heritage over time, despite being so close to the Western culture of Panama City."

Technique:

Though this station presents theme writing across three scenarios, in reality, they often overlap. At the following station, we cover the interpretive framework methodology which combines all three levels as seen in this photo from Chagres National Park in Panama. Here the

The small committee for Chagres National Park contemplates how to convert emerging themes into interpretive themes. See the following station for the final themes in English.

community produces the emerging themes, later refined by the small committee (photo), and finally written by a single person who executes the committee's consensus mandate. The methodology reflects the reality that large groups work best to generate Big Ideas and set the bounds of discussion while small groups and individuals function best for writing.

I also share a more historic example of this interaction in the US *Declaration of Independence:* "We hold these truths to be self-evident, that all men are created equal, that they are endowed by their Creator with certain unalienable Rights, that among these are Life, Liberty and the pursuit of Happiness."

This famous theme statement from the *Declaration* fully represents this section's main points. While written directly by the hand of Thomas Jefferson (individual), he served on a five-member committee to draft the document (team). But the ideas in the *Declaration* originate from a community of colonial states and in fact reflect a recognition of universal human rights emerging not just in America, but across Europe. Consequently, the resulting theme and *Declaration* were completely adopted by the colonial community so much so that many patriots died in the attempt to implement the *Declaration's* principles and goal of independence. What more could an interpreter ask for!

All levels share the need to document the theme in order to make it accountable and editable. I say "document" and not necessarily "write" owing to the pathbreaking work by Carlos Rosero in Colombia who works with subliterate rural fishing populations. There he discovered that themes and presentations are best recorded and played back on cell phones rather than on paper. Either way, even if you write alone, you should want feedback. If the theme remains hidden in your mind, it remains likewise impervious to serious feedback and improvement by others.

Several benefits also can result from the meeting of minds. First, if a team takes on the task of writing up the site's themes, people from different divisions and professions can offer a richer diversity of inputs and ideas into the theme creation process. Second, the more people that participate—even though coordination costs increase—the greater the ownership for resulting themes. If more people feel ownership, the absorption and use of themes accelerate avoiding the ever-common problem of contradictory messaging from different sides of the organization. When the community becomes involved and feels ownership, the themes may show up in private sector use, in local government, museums, and other venues that together reinforce each other in the eyes of visitors and of the world.

Role of the Professional Writer in Theme Writing

In modern society, we outsource so many of our jobs. The interpretive world proves no exception. You can outsource everything including the planning, writing, designing, fabrication, and delivery of personal media. Consultants bustle about waiting for your call.

In the case of theme writing, professional consultant writers usually cannot replace the interpreter and content experts or heritage community needed to develop a Big Idea. In fact, the more an outsider produces, the more ownership remains in his or her hands and not in those of those who actually have to implement. In this sense, writers can backfire if used incorrectly. Professional writers, on the other hand, serve best as part of an interpretive team. This way the team may outsource the actual writing but not their own thinking, hopefully maintaining Big Idea ownership with those who "own" the heritage and must implement the interpretation. We also argue that an interpretive professional in our modern world should develop the skill to not just create themes that excite them but work with groups and communities to develop appropriate themes for greater uses.

Putting Together a Theme Team

For interpretive programs, institutional interpreters often write alone but request feedback from colleagues and need approval from supervisors. Freelance interpretive tour guides may literally write alone without consulting anyone. For non-personal media, a team almost always drives development whether in-house or out-sourced. Whom to incorporate in such teams depends on whose power is required to make the interpretation happen and whose ideas should dominate. In the unfortunate reality, heritage sites often leave interpreters to their means without sufficient support. The following letter is for interpreters who need to convince their supervisors to offer adequate support. Please modify the letter on the opposite page to your case, whether you present the argument verbally or in writing.

Writing as a Theme Team

This *Field Guide* and the Interpretive Theme Writer's Worksheet guide an individual interpreter through the theme writing process. In Station 7, we will discuss how you facilitate a community-based interpretive framework. For now, then, we talk briefly about writing as a theme team, or if you and your colleagues are really good, as a dream theme team.

In writing, many roads lead to Rome. Your route depends on how many people participate, their skill levels, experience working together, project urgency, individual dynamics, etc. These steps, therefore, you might consider merely as a starting point.

1. Choose a topic, which depends as we saw at Station 2 on management objectives, heritage qualities, visitor interests, and your own knowledge and motivation. Write it on a board.

2. Brainstorm elements that might contribute to a potential theme. Multiple methodologies exist, including writing down everything that comes to mind, having people use cards and grouping them, a group mind map, etc. Hopefully as a team you have already done this, otherwise, you can also see at the next station one technique that works for teams, communities, or any kind of group.

3. Hand out the Interpretive Theme Writer's Worksheet and have everyone write a theme that they like (the primary audience).

4. Have a session to compare and combine or choose.

5. Then have the best writer or at least the nominated writer produce a first draft and put that on the Theme Team Round Robin Worksheet.

6. Rotate the theme draft and get feedback.

7. Write a second draft and do it again.

8. Write a third draft.

9. Once final and approved, you can derive a secondary theme for whichever secondary audiences you may have.

Date

Mrs. X
Interpretive Supervisor
State Park

Dear Mrs. X:

The challenges to managing heritage are many. Overtourism, for instance, has become increasingly discussed in recent years. One way to convert that potentially large impact into a large benefit is through an effective interpretation program. Interpretation not only increases the visitor experience by provoking visitors to think more deeply and create more connections between their own background, experience, and values with the heritage that we manage, but it also can motivate them to take actions that favor heritage conservation such as give donations, volunteer, advertise by word-of-mouth, share contacts, all depending on what we ask of them.

Central to effective interpretation are the interpretive themes that we write. More so than other forms of communication that package their messages to be delivered, interpretation presents a theme that the audience develops and builds on in its own mind, understanding it according to their background. A strong theme not only helps us to focus our program design by choosing only materials that support the theme, but a theme likewise helps visitors to focus and understand how the information we present all fits together. The idea is to choose a theme that not only provokes them to think but it is easy to process and understand.

For this to work requires participation of several people. Aside from just the interpreter (me), it requires managers to approve budgets for material procurement, architects to build infrastructure reflective of themes, designers for the exhibits, experts to ensure the contents. It requires wildlife biologists to identify projects that we want interpretation to support. It requires financial managers to set up donation reception and accounting systems. It requires the superintendent who speaks about our heritage to the public to base her comments on the same themes as we use with the public. It often even requires local residents whose ideas about our place are key to their supporting us through visitation, helping out, and offering political support. Alone the interpreter (me), can fill very few of these roles needed for success.

For these reasons, I would like to request that X, Y, and Z persons work with me to develop the interpretive themes for (the park/exhibit/visitor center/program) and any necessary systems and materials to move those themes to action. Without good interpretive programming, we often find ourselves on the defensive before the arrival of visitors rather than proactively figure out how they can help us do our jobs better.

Thank you very much for your consideration.

Your Humble Interpreter

Station 6 Big Ideas

1. Themes can emerge as readily from teams and communities as individual theme writers.

2. Multiple minds can produce not only richer themes but ones for which ownership is more broadly shared.

3. Professional writers can complement a team, but the team should only outsource the writing, not the thinking.

STATION 6 EXERCISE

Answers to station exercises can be found in the Field Notes starting on page 115.

Convert the Big Idea into a strong interpretive theme.

Big Idea	Strong Interpretive Theme
Geologically, Native Americans are as much visitors as Europeans are.	
On the map, Australia is no more down under than Russia.	
Growth is the measure of both macroeconomic progress and doom.	
The goal is to die in the largest, most encompassing paradigm/worldview possible.	
Name your own	

Theme Notes

Interpretive Frameworks Leverage the Power of Community for Interpretation

Meanings and Heritage Are Central to Community Development
The PUP Consortium has been helping protected heritage areas to develop their own interpretive themes since 1998 with Pico Bonito National Park in Honduras (I would not consider these strong themes today. Why do you think I say that?):

1. Pico Bonito National Park, one of the biggest in Honduras, presents an exceptional panoramic view of steep slopes reaching great altitudes close to the sea.

2. Pico Bonito has a high percentage of those life zones found in Honduras owing to its vertical stratification and extensive territory.

3. Pico Bonito produces water for a half million people in three states in the north of the country.

4. For hundreds of years, the Tolupan people have been living in the southeast sector of Pico Bonito. There are also characteristics of the Yaruca people, which has been losing its history.

5. Pico Bonito's history has many myths and legends from La Ceiba and Pico Bonito itself.

6. Pico Bonito's natural resource conservation has been positively and negatively impacted by agriculture and agroforestry.

7. Pico Bonito National Park is the strongest link in the most fragile sector of the Mesoamerican Biological Corridor that runs from México to Panamá.

We started the theme creation process by developing simple sets of separate-but-equal themes. Over time, our theme concept evolved into an interpretive framework, based distantly on the 1936 National Park Service concept of a "thematic framework." At first we worked just with park employees, but since we now facilitate community-based, consensus-building processes with local stakeholders. Early framework versions consisted of hierarchically organized themes, such as the example below from the Valle de Oro National Wildlife Refuge in New Mexico. Eventually we integrated other essential heritage elements necessary to fully experience a site's heritage (thanks to the writing of Steve Van Matre), including universal processes and essence (or *genius loci*, as architects often say) as seen in the Flint Hills example (also below). No doubt the model will continue to evolve.

At UNESCO, we believe there is no choice to make between saving lives and saving cultural heritage. Protecting heritage is inseparable from protecting populations, because heritage enshrines people's identities. Heritage gives people strength and confidence to look to the future—it is a force for social cohesion and recovery. This is why protection of heritage must be an integral part of all humanitarian efforts.

Irina Bokova

Our understanding of how to use heritage meanings has also grown from simply an input into tourism product design to an essential element of community development and recovery (see marginal quote by the former secretary general of UNESCO). We reason that for communities to take ownership of their heritage and invest in its development and conservation, their views and meanings of that heritage should be recognized and honored. But often they never have the opportunity or space to think about or articulate those meanings, those Big Ideas, let alone strong interpretive themes. The interpretive framework process affords them that opportunity.

We built that methodology on top of the facilitation process called the Workshop Method of the Technology of Participation, created by the venerable, international, grassroots non-profit, Institute for Cultural Affairs. Essentially it guides groups through brainstorming, to small group refinement, to plenary organizing and naming, to small committee writing that converts emergent themes into interpretive themes. Ultimately these themes become property of the community which includes the protected area. Their use over time should strengthen community self-esteem and self-worth, especially in those communities whose heritage has not received much visitation or attention. The interpretive planner facilitates community understanding of their own heritage more deeply which serves as the foundation for all interpretive planning and tourism product development thereafter. In this sense, interpretive planning draws a direct economic connection between heritage meanings and economic income.

Despite the interpretive literature's focus on individual theme writing, most if not all ideas already belong to the human collective field of consciousness, though we often perceive ourselves as separate (see quotes by quantum physicist David Bohm and the theme about themes Theme Spotlight in this *Field Guide's* introduction). Now we offer a collective process to express those collective ideas.

Why We Use Interpretive Frameworks

1. They connect heritage with meanings and processes, provoking thinking and appreciation.

2. Different but related themes reinforce each other, forging new relationships.

3. All communications at an institution use the same themes in the same way to avoid mis- and cross-communication problems.

4. Planners choose which theme best fits a given audience.

5. Themes and their associated heritage elements facilitate the work of tour guides and operators, historians, students, government officials, and residents.

6. With publicly sanctioned themes, unscrupulous heritage recreation providers cannot simply make up meanings and stories to entertain their paying patrons.

7. A framework lends interpretation a structure to plan and build experience opportunities for guests to deepen appreciation for a place.

8. They serve as the heart of any interpretive or heritage management plan.

9. They reinforce the notion that themes alone are insufficient basis for heritage interpretation. There are other equally important elements, all of which interact.

10. They create a space in which community value notions of heritage are articulated and honored.

> Thought is a system belonging to the whole culture and society, evolving over history, and it creates the image of an individual who is supposed to be the source of thought.
>
> I think one of the fundamental mistakes of the human race has been to say that when you have finished with a thought, it's gone. But it hasn't gone—it has 'folded back' into the rest of consciousness.
>
> *David Bohm*

Valle de Oro National Wildlife Refuge (VdO) Interpretive Framework[i]

Overarching message prepared by the small committee — Universal forces and process

An evolving participatory stewardship model aims to balance the complexity of nature with that of modern life.

Description: Nature's complexity manifests in the structure of forests, diversity of river life, variety of habitat types, and the development of social organization, high-order thinking, and consciousness. Modern complexity manifests in sophisticated governance, interrelated communication and economic flows, and the diversity of cultural and spiritual expression. Evolution in fact tends toward greater complexity, but at times can be set back locally by powerful natural phenomena like tsunamis and volcanic eruptions. It can also be set back by uncontrolled economic growth and industrial output that transform natural complexity into human complexity. An emerging vision of a healthy balance of human and non-human complexities, however, necessitates a new stewardship model that emphasizes active collaboration of all levels of society with traditional decision-makers. VdO is just such a place where this evolving model takes shape, where nature's complexity co-exists and blends with the urban complexity of modern life.

Universal messages prepared by the small committee — Universal forces and process

Migration and cultivation, traditionally guided by natural cycles, have been fragmented by modern transportation and production systems creating complex landscape mosaics.	When people come together to connect with and care for the land, they heal the environment and themselves.	Due to evolving social awareness and activism, protected areas must now work in deeper collaboration with their communities, requiring a new participatory conservation stewardship model.
Description: Migration and cultivation date thousands or millions of years (if one includes ant fungal cultivation, for example), guided entirely by natural cycles. In industrial times, modern thinking has invented linear time, where processes are seen as having beginnings, middles, and ends, where materials start at a source and end in a sink, where problems are black and white, where A leads to B to C and do not cycle back. This thinking has subdued awareness of natural cycles and can been seen in the landscape with production and transportation systems. While some criticize replacement of cyclical time with linear, the blend enhances landscape complexity (forest remnants co-exist with industrial ruin, bike paths, and heritage areas). Ultimately these complex landscape mosaics contribute to place identity. VdO will show this combination of dairy-agricultural history with habitat and visitor use diversity.	**Description:** Human deprivation and abuse very often relate directly to the land, whether abuses take the form of water pollution, loss of access to green spaces, being sequestered into small spaces, cut off from heritage pasts, deprived of traditional foods and practices, etc. These deprivations weaken the body, mind, and social networks that maintain cultures. By coming together to restore the environment, people not only clean the sources of their own sustenance, both physical and psychological, but also build and strengthen social bonds between those coming together, whether simply planting a tree or organizing to fight industrial pollution and mindsets that oppress minorities, including the land. VdO is situated in a historic hotspot of environmental injustice, and its presence and mission not only bring the community to heal the land, but in so doing heal the social fabric of the South Valley community itself.	**Description:** Society and the world evolve in many ways including social awareness, activism, technologically, proliferation of information sources and democratization, number of NGOs and interest groups, etc. Where before protected area agencies both planned and implemented unilaterally, today, they are compelled, at times willingly or grudgingly, to collaborate with their communities (defined broadly) to include interest groups wherever they may be found. This collaboration requires a new model only just now emerging and characterized by greater participation, power redistribution, innovation, agility, and learning VdO for instance pioneers urban refuge standards, multiple channels of community participation, participatory interpretation as a fundamental design criterion for layout and programming, partnerships with AMAFCA's stormwater drainage system and many other organizations.

Local messages prepared by the small committee — Combination of unique aspects or forces

Throughout time, people and other species migrate along the Rio Grande because of water availability according to natural cycles.	Pueblo, Hispano, European, and modern industrial methods of cultivation have blended through time to produce a mosaic of agricultural systems in the MRGV, including modern habitat restoration.	The environmental justice movement in the South Valley heals land and people through VdO.	VdO creates and cares for an accessible gallery of Middle Rio Grande habitats.	VdO evolves from and for its urban community.	VdO pioneers a community-based model for integrating cultural and natural heritage in protected landscapes.

Interpretive Framework for Valle de Oro National Wildlife Refuge, Albuquerque, New Mexico.

Major Steps to Facilitate Interpretive Frameworks

An entire book describes the full use and facilitation of the Workshop Method (*The Workshop Book: From Individual Creativity to Group Action*). Practitioners can also take a two-day training workshop to become a certified user of the methodology. So the following major steps decidedly remain brief given the impossibility of including all the details that contribute to quality outcomes. I recommend that you download the PUP methodological manual from the PUP Consortium website (pupconsortium.net/focusareas/pup/manual/), which shares many more details on how to apply the generic version of this workshop. The figures in this section show the major steps in the process.

It is worth mentioning that the methodology often includes what the Institute calls a Historic Scan (see

Site Planning for Life

Managing Visitors for Heritage Destinations

Manual for PUP Core Planning Teams

The Flint Hills landscape undulates through space, burns through time, and offers refuge to its ever changing character of community.					

The undulating limestone and tallgrass prairie landscape of the Flint Hills traces the submarine surface of an ancient inland sea, 165 million years ago.		The Flint Hill's ecologic and agropastoral patterns dance to cycles of human-induced fire.	In recent centuries, the Flint Hills have suffered various displacements of its (non)human inhabitants, leaving behind fragmented communities, but enriching its overall natural and cultural diversity.		
The precipitation of minerals exposed to prolonged periods of pressure produces sedimentary rocks such as limestone from calcium carbonate skeletons of marine organisms.	As tectonic plates move about the surface of the earth, their collisions produce uplift into mountains and creation of new land surfaces.	Complex dynamic systems, such as fire-dependent ecosystems, cycle through stages of rapid growth, conservation, and then rapid energy release that feeds the next cycle.	Economic growth converts land uses, leaving behind patches of the pre-existing use, such as natural habitats.	Species expand into areas of low relative competition, often displacing existing residents.	The rise and fall of cultural practices depends on the socio-economic needs of the times.
Sedimentary rock formation, tectonic uplift	Tectonic uplift, plate movement	Dynamic conservation cycle of replenishment	Economic activity and habitat fragmentation	Colonization and displacement	Rise and fall of cultural practices and icons
Millions of years of pressure crushed calcium carbonate animal skeletons into limestone at the bottom of an inland sea, later uplifted by tectonic activity into today's viewscape of the Flint Hills.	The undulating surface of an ancient inland seabed has risen and transformed into a sea of tallgrass prairie.	Despite the destructive power of fire, without it, trees and shrubs would overgrow and smother the productive tallgrass prairie.	The Flint Hills is the largest intact block of remaining tallgrass prairie, capable of sustaining viable populations of prairie chickens.	Fort Riley was the lance point into Kaw territory to move and protect settlers from the East into the future slave-free Kansas and beyond.	The rise of the iconic cowboy culture depended as much on the quality of the Flint Hill tallgrass prairie and railroad access, as it did on the cows themselves.
• Large concentration of marine fossils	• High-rated clear sunsets and sunrises	• Deep roots	Prairie chickens	• Last aboriginal homeland of Kaw Nation • First territorial Capitol of Kansas • First US case of Spanish Flu in Fort Riley • First land-grant college in the US	• Iconic cowboy

ramework does not include examples of the following heritage elements: intangible expressions and outstanding features.

rpretive Framework for the Flint Hills Discovery Center, Manhattan, Kansas

Theme Spotlight at this station). In this context, the facilitator leads a scan of the site's history by creating a site timeline and from that draws forth raw materials for the second activity to construct the interpretive framework. We will not describe the Historic Scan here but again the steps can be found in the manual.

Finally, you can use this approach at any scale. We have created interpretive frameworks for the moon at the largest scale as well as the Portuguese Discoverers as they spread out across the world during their Golden Age. On the other end, Valle de Oro is only 488 acres, but we could create a framework for a single house if such were the need.

Preparation

Agree with stakeholders on the value of an interpretive framework and a commitment to implement it

Recruit and invite 15 to 30 stakeholders to a workshop (9–4 pm) that should be carried out more than once to accommodate different schedules and to ensure a diverse community representation

See the PUP manual for details on materials preparation

Introduction

Begin with an icebreaker

Introduce interpretive frameworks and the project context

Universal processes

Have participants identify for each emerging theme the universal processes represented by that theme or contributed to what the discusses

Emerging themes

Ask participants to individually brainstorm significant attributes about the site's heritage based on provided examples

Break individuals into four small groups which then select among their ideas the 10 best options which they write on cards

Have the small groups return to the plenary but remain together

Ask (the facilitator) the small groups for the three best, clearest cards to place on the wall

Interview the cards to determine their consensus meanings

Pair cards according to new ideas that connect them, not just similarity of words

Ask groups to put up three cards with ideas not currently represented on the wall

Interview those cards

Group cards in two or more always looking for new relationships for the site

Place remaining cards on wall, adding to or modifying groups. Cards can also remain alone. This results in four to seven groups of at least three cards each.

Begin with the largest group, write a title that represents the idea trying to emerge from the group of cards. It should contain four to seven words.

Repeat for remaining groups of three or more cards. These titles are the emerging themes.

Look for relationships among the themes and record any results.

Interpretive themes and essence

Convene a small writing committee of six people

Present what is an interpretive theme

The committee transforms the emerging themes into interpretive ones. It may create higher-order themes in a hierarchical relation. Refine the writing.

Review the processes and extract the essence

Write two- to three-paragraph descriptions for each theme, shorter descriptions for the processes and essence to accompany the framework (see example below).

Proceedings and Conclusion

Write the proceedings and present the draft framework to the plenary as soon as possible. Ask for feedback.

The small committee integrates comments and distributes the draft to the general community.

The committee may receive additional comments and create a final, third draft.

Later the framework can be used to design experience opportunities, products, and even experience zoning.

Theme Descriptions

Since the framework design allows a reader to see the entire framework and the relationships between its elements on one page in one view, additional descriptions and justifications of elements follow on subsequent pages. Each theme should have an accompanying description of at least two or three paragraphs that captures main points, elaborations, and evidence for each theme. For example:

Valle de Oro National Wildlife Refuge Theme
"An evolving participatory stewardship model aims to balance the complexity of nature with that of modern life."

Description: "Nature's complexity takes shape in the structure of forests, diversity of river life, variety of habitat types, and the development of social organization, high-order thinking, and consciousness. Modern complexity takes shape in sophisticated governance, interrelated communication and economic flows, and the diversity of cultural and spiritual expression. Evolution in fact tends toward greater complexity, but at times can be set back locally by powerful natural phenomena like tsunamis and volcanic eruptions. It can also be set back by uncontrolled economic growth and industrial output that transform natural complexity into human complexity. An emerging vision of a healthy balance of human and non-human complexities, however, requires a new stewardship model that emphasizes active collaboration of all levels of society with traditional decision-makers. VdO is just such a place where this evolving model emerges, where nature's complexity co-exists and blends with the urban complexity of modern life."

CATIE Theme
"From the University to the Field: Socioenvironmental problems cannot be solved from a university campus; they require both virtual and physical extension to communities in order to generate and transfer knowledge, both academic and community-based."

Description: "For centuries, the great universities have erected their buildings in the hearts of metropolitan areas, enjoying privileges that flow from civilization. But with the increase in the dynamic complexity of challenges emerging today requires that universities leave behind the ancient concept of ivory towers and look to extend and integrate themselves with other forms of knowledge especially local in order to transcend problems that grow increasingly resistant."

THEME SPOTLIGHT: HISTORICAL SCAN SUPPORTS THEME IDENTIFICATION

Timeline:

The facilitation of a historical scan or time line generates not only pride in constructing a consensus understanding of the place's history but ideas and elements that will be used to generate themes, universal processes, and heritage elements later in the process.

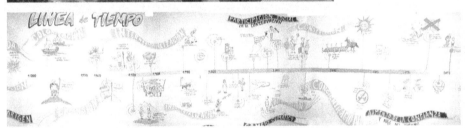

A graphic reporter rendered the time line seen on the wall into a visually attractive version.

Technique:

Though we do not discuss the historical scan technique in detail in this Field Guide, the exercise which precedes the emerging theme workshop involves the audience's creation of a site timeline divided into historical periods. From this exercise, not only do participants generate heritage elements that can be used later to populate theme descriptions, but historical periods themselves can offer clues to actual themes. The activity also motivates participants as the product contains a high dose of visual Vitamin R for them, setting the scene for the following activity described at this station.

The example comes from the Tayrona National Park interpretive framework exercise in Colombia. A graphic reporter has converted the timeline as it appears on the wall behind the PUP Consortium facilitation team in card form to the final product that appears in the proceedings and interpretive plan.

Interpretive Framework Format Can Reflect Additional Meaning

This methodology encourages meaning creation at each step along the way. This also includes the actual the framework's graphical layout which at its best should provoke through its relevant imagery and processing ease. Most interpretive frameworks use the standard table layout seen in examples above. But others have been more creative and meaningful. For example, the framework for the Illinois River Valley outside of Chicago lays the framework out using imagery of the Illinois River snaking through cornfields.

For Tayrona National Park's framework, the same graphic reporter team rendered it in real time into an artwork. The essence beats at the drawing's heart from which universal processes emanate outwards toward the interpretive themes, each decorated with a descriptive image. While this format probably does not contribute much additional information about the park's meaning, it remains to be seen if an attractive, graphical format actually improves audience engagement with the framework.

Station 7 Big Ideas

1. Interpretive frameworking is a methodology and product to capture community perspective and understanding of heritage as well as build community ownership and pride in and management of that heritage.

2. Heritage contributes to a community's identity and thus its self-esteem and self-image, which embody a potential for the community to develop or recover from problems.

3. Interpretive frameworks connect interpretive planning to a community development process.

4. To fully experience and appreciate a site's heritage, visitors must experience its essence, understand the universal processes that created it and continue to transform it, think about its interpretive themes, and visit and know the heritage elements that define the place.

5. The framework format itself can provide additional insight and meaning into the heritage beyond words that compose it.

Great Transformations: Connecting Great Lakes to Great Rivers

The forested ribbon of the Illinois River meanders through horizon-hugging corn fields and tallgrass prairie before that, belying the geological, cultural, commercial, and ecological transformations of water flow that began thousands of years ago when glaciers bumped west the Mississippi River, to last century's cross-continental connections of Great Lakes and Great Rivers, to today's wildlife restoration along farmed-over floodplains.

Geological Transformations: Carving a New Watershed
Beneath the Illinois River's flowing waters lie two glacier-transformed beds. Seventeen thousand years ago, Wisconsin Glacier melt water burst a rock-earth dam holding back a massive lake and released the Kankakee Torrent that over weeks dug the river valley all the way to Hennepin; there flood waters caromed south into the dry riverbed of the ancient Mississippi, emptied itself when, millennia earlier, the Kansas Glacier pushed the river west to its current course.

17,000 years ago

Lightning Birth
The Kankakee Torrent carved the Illinois River in a geological lightning bolt of time, thereby commencing a series of landscape transformations emanating from the valley.

- Ridge near present-day Kankakee
- Starved Rock
- Buffalo Rock
- Big Bend
- Great Falls

A New Frontier
The formation of the valley created a new riparian habitat that allowed the eastern woodland a foothold farther west than before, essentially shifting the prairie land-wood land frontier in the Prairie State.

12,000 years ago

- Best exemplary site and its founding
- McNaughton Park or Sandy Ford Natural Area or Buffalo Rock SP or Warnecke Woods?
- McCune Sand Prairie

Commercial Transformations: Hub of North America
In 150 years, Illinoisans had transformed the Illinois River from America's most productive inland fishery into America's cross-continental transportation hub, connecting the Great Lakes, Mississippi River, and Gulf of Mexico by means of canals, dams, locks, and even the reversed flow of the Chicago River.

150 years ago

Good Fishing Not Enough
Despite the Illinois River Valley's having been the most productive inland fishery in the United States, society opted instead to sacrifice that productivity if necessary in place of industrialization and commerce.

- Mussels for buttons and pearls
- Best bass from southern LaGrange Reach
- Banner Marsh

Great Cross-Continental Connection
Through a series of canals, dams, and locks, the Illinois River linked the Great Lakes and Mississippi River, essentially creating not only North America's transportation hub at Chicago, but the only cross-continental shipping access from Canada to the Gulf of Mexico.

- Illinois & Michigan Canal connects Chicago and Illinois Rivers, America's first National Heritage Corridor in 1984
- Chicago Sanitary and Ship Canal took over from the Michigan & Illinois Canal
- Illinois Waterway
- Reversal of Chicago River connects Illinois River with Great Lakes
- Hennepin Canal connects Illinois and Mississippi Rivers
- Marseilles Locks
- Spirit of Peoria steamboat

Changing the Channel
The Illinois River has been dredged, narrowed, dammed, leveed, and pumped in the interest of navigability, agricultural industrialization, and flood control. Ironically in some cases, these measures combined with loss of backwater lakes and siltation worsened floods.

- Largest project to dredge and narrow?
- Place where levee may have broken?
- 1 particular flood worsened by measures?

Near future

Cultural Transformations: 500 Generations of Settlement
For 500 generations, since Native Americans first arrived to the are 12,000 years ago, settlers have diverted Illinois River waters to eve more uses -- fishing, exploration, agriculture, fur trapping, waste removal, industrial cooling, recreation, and habitat restoration -- ea time not only adding functionality to the river's flow, but transform: its meaning.

Birthplace of American Archeology
From early Clovis settlers to the great city of Cahokia, the Illinois River Valley and the neighboring Mississippi 3 river valley essentially transformed the field of archeology in the United States both in history and in the sheer numbers of sites excavated.

- Dickson Mounds
- Cahokia World Heritage Site
- Fort Crevecoeur Park

A Place to Visit
For the past three centuries, settlers and urbanites alike have arrived attracted by the region's productivity and beauty.

- William Boyce and founding of Boy Scouts of America in Ottawa
- Washington Square, first Lincoln-Douglas debate in Ottawa, 1858
- French explorers, loosely connect Joliet and Marquette Expedition
- The Plow Creek Mennonite Community
- Donnelley Depue State Fish & Wildlife Area, migratory bird stopover or Chautauqua NWR
- Grandview Drive, Peoria

Just Another Input
For much of the 20th Century, people tre the river as merely an industrial or urban input, rather than a waterway of spiritual ecological value.

- Reversed Chicago River to carry sewage and wastes away from the city
- Marseilles Locks that bypass Great Falls

Today

Ecological Transformations: Power of the Floodpulse
For millennia the Illinois River's cyclical floodpulses energized floodplains with biodiversity and ecological production; but then industrialization and urbanization furrowed floodplains and backwater lakes into corn fie injected exotics like zebra mussel and Asian carp, and befouled waters with wastes. Citizens, however, eventu began to restore the water's health and the floodpulse's seasonal rhythm so that the River may again flow with ecological splendor and even become an international model for floodplain restoration.

Tightening the Corn Belt
The advance of corn and other crops not only eliminated great swaths of prairie but also habitats such as backwater lakes home to many terrestrial animals as well as fish, effectively encircling the riparian ribbon of the Illinois River.

- Creative agriculture as response to overdependence on dominant corn crop??? (Is this true?)
- Emiquon National Wildlife Refuge

Circulatory Problem
Just as the heart cyclically pumps a "bloodpulse" to carry nutrients throughout the body, the Illinois River cyclically pumps its floodpulse to carry nutrients throughout its floodplains. Limiting this millennial flow reduced and eliminated many habitats in the river's floodplains.

- Locks and dams excluded summer drying of Illinois River
- Levees cut off half floodplains restricting fish from spawning grounds
- Banner Marsh

Restoration for the World
This river system has shown extraordinary resilience, so much that conservationists are not only restoring some of the Illinois's floodplains but even considering it, along with upper Mississippi River restoration efforts, a possible international model for floodplain restoration.

- Nation Research Council's 1992 verdict that Illinois River was one of only 3 river systems in US that has potential for significant restoration
- Clean Water Act reduced pollution significantly and comeback of fish and mussels
- Restoration at Emiquon, largest backwater lake restoration project as well as floodpulse
- Restoration and possible reconnection of Spunky Bottoms to the Illinois River
- Local farmers on Mackinaw River restoration project
- Restored tallgrass prairie at Matheson State Park, McHune Sand Prairie
- Dam silt build up rejuvenates islands and mudflats similar to original pre-dam river (Peoria Lake)
- Battling exotics: Zebra mussel from Great Lakes and Asian Carp from the Mississippi (during 1993 Mississippi River floods)
- Restored strip mine at Mautino State Fish and Wildlife Area
- LaFayette Home Nursery (prairie restoration)
- Hennepin and Hopper Lake Restoration Project (wetlands restoration)

Illinois River Valley Interpretive Framework

FERMA
play, learn,

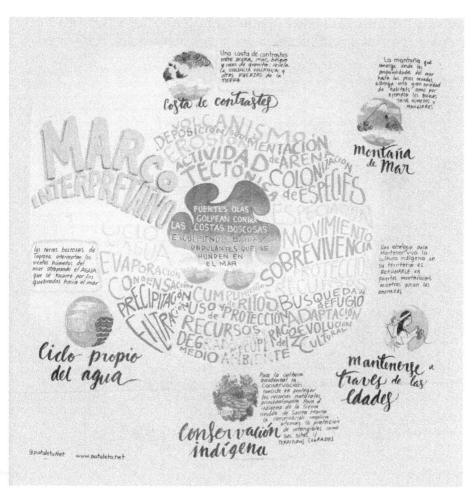

This interpretive framework for Colombia's Tayrona National Park rendered by a graphic reporter shows the essence in the middle of surrounded by universal processes with the themes orbiting around along with the icons.

At left: This framework comes from an earlier generation marked by hierarchically related themes with the overarching theme at the top (Great Transformations) that binds all other themes such as the sub-themes (Geological Transformations) divided into storylines (Lightning Birth) with examples of stories and specific locations with bullet points.

THEME SPOTLIGHT: RELATING EMERGENT THEMES TO CONSTRUCT AN OVERALL SITE STORY OR THEME

Emergent Themes:

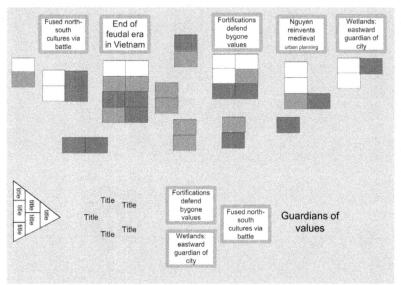

This set of theme cards represent an interpretive framework workshop for all of Viet Nam with representatives from UNESCO sites in different parts of the countries. After developing emerging themes in the blue boxes, participants organized the emerging themes to extract yet more meaning by identifying relationships between them.

Technique:

One facet of deeper appreciation depends on the interrelation of heritage elements and ideas. That is, you should not be satisfied with a series of separate themes, each covering a distinct dominion of a site's heritage. If those themes can be related and connected to show that all heritage elements emanate from the same universal processes, a visitor can more deeply understand what has happened and continues to occur there. For this reason, when the plenary has developed a series of emergent themes, the facilitator lines them up and seeks to extract additional relationships and meanings.

The example above comes from a practice interpretive framework exercise for the entire country of Viet Nam, designed to accommodate a mixed audience of heritage site managers from three distinct sites. When they combined emergent themes, it became clear that three themes clearly referred to efforts to guard traditional values. If facilitators had completed the process, they could have derived an overall theme or title based on this confluence of meaning.

STATION 7 EXERCISES

Answers to station exercises can be found in the Field Notes starting on page 115.

Exercise 1: Place the following components from the interpretive framework of Chagres National Park in Panama into the following framework table.

Chagres River	**Intersection of Biodiversity:** A well conserved forest is genetically strengthened and strengthens other forests through direct connectivity.
Conquest and rebirth	
Cultural assimilation	
Dense forest harvests clouds and rain, pumping them along the Chagres River	Lowest cloud forest in Central America
Dispersion	Panama Canal
Emberá Drúa Village	Royal Road
From the Ancient Road to the Modern Royal Road: The same Camino Real (Royal Road) that connected interoceanic and prehispanic commerce became the principal route for the Spanish colonization that extracted gold from the New World and sent it to the Old, thus paving the way for rural and urban settlement in the center of Panama.	**Safe Distance:** Although Western culture impacted the heritage of many indigenous people, the Emberá have conserved their heritage over time, despite being so close to Western culture.
	Solar energy maintains civilization
	Succession and migration
	Water cycle (Foehm Effect)
Harpy eagle	**Water Passage:** Chagres National Park does not only contribute 40 percent of the water for the Panama Canal and for the consumption of 1.7 million people, but also contributes to Panama's national image.
Interoceanic Communication: The Chagres River communicates between oceans via commerce, cultures, and even genes	

Essence						
Universal processes						
Integrated theme						
Local themes						
Heritage elements						

Exercise 2: Integrate Themes into Higher-Level Themes

As with the example in the above exercise and that of Valle de Oro earlier at this station, you can integrate local themes or those that come from the workshop into a higher-level theme that transcends and includes its components. You may do this if it adds considerable value or if participants do it intuitively during a workshop. The example below comes from El Cocuy National Park in Colombia where participants created universal themes from local themes. The two on the left are both cultural while the two on the right are natural. Try to create your own universal themes based on the given local themes.

Universal Themes	Throwing Salt on the Sacred Wound _____ _____ _____		Glaciations and Biodiversity _____ _____ _____	
Local Themes	**The Salt Route** Commercial traffic along the Salt Route, whether indigenous or Spanish, drove the cultural and territorial domination of El Cocuy and its surroundings.	**Desecration** Despite the fact that the Spanish brought the Holy Cross to extend their religion over the indigenous cosmovision, in reality, they desecrated their land.	**Glacial Masses** Although the snowcap mountains of Güicán, Cocuy and Chita have one of the most extensive glacial masses north of the equator, the peaks that were once covered in ice, one by one, are melting.	**Biodiversity and Endemism** Given the altitudinal gradient that cuts across extensive forests and paramos and the resulting abundance of habitat, El Cocuy National Park is the heart of high levels of biodiversity and endemism, such as the (*Frailejón Epeletia cleffi*) and collard lizard (*Stenocercus lache*).

Theme Notes

Interpretive Intelligence Can Defend Against Artificial Intelligence

Though theme writing might seem an eternally relevant skill forged from the cauldron of the very first alphabets more than five millennia ago, useful until the day we no longer produce content for our exhibits, signage, and Instagram accounts. Let's hope that day never comes. But, alas, such self-interested security may be but a mirage with the rise of artificial intelligence. Indeed, technology has already been busily replacing many positions formerly occupied by flesh-and-blood workers, whether assembling cars in factories, dispensing money in banks, mining minerals, driving taxis, or—I lament to reveal—guiding.

Aside from the heralded fictional guides that we find in *Star Wars* such as the eminent C3PO capable of speaking six million dialects or those customer-service bots that lull human space travelers into obesity and atrophy in *Wall-E,* real manifestations of both artificial intelligence and robots now invade our profession. Telepresence robots represent a rapidly growing industry having deployed numerous robots into the field such as FROG in Sevilla, Spain, the Smithsonian's Pepper the Robot (see picture), or remote-controlled robots at the American Museum of Natural History in New York City.

Artificial intelligence can now write formulaic articles for newspapers, give speeches on New York City buses, detect human facial expressions and modify its responses, pass the Turing Test, beat chess masters, outperform highly educated professionals in making data-intensive predictions, and the disembodied Siri and Alexa already haunt the smart phones of millions of people who long for a mild-mannered guide to lead them around the Internet. I hesitate even to pen these examples knowing that they will quickly date this *Field Guide* as new and more impressive telepresent guide-bots roll off robot-operated assembly lines. I may well have to contract an AI consulting service to write a field guide of robotic museum and nature guides in the near future.

I say all this not to throw a sheet-metal jacket of gloom over you. The world already does this well enough without my help. I mention it because the first interpreters to lose their jobs are those who don't create, just execute. That is the province of early AI. But those who will lose their jobs last will be those who can master the highest faculties of mind to design opportunities that provoke heritage-visiting humans into new awareness. Central to that pursuit stands tall the art and craft of interpretive theme writing. For the time being, the apex of interpretation revolves around the development and presentation of transformational Big Ideas, taking best advantage of human psychology in ways that only *Homo sapiens* can understand. Writing themes is hard business, and I couldn't even imagine how an AI programmer—who would have to be a whiz theme writer him- or herself and if so would not likely be a programmer—could write an algorithm to come up with Big Ideas that depend so much on human experience as well as high levels of awareness and cognition that can synthesize and make connections across terabytes of possible choices.

So make yourself irreplaceable in the interpretation world, in the museum world, in the parks world, and build your skills to write themes. Just like a bird field guide can only show you the birds but cannot find them for you, this *Field Guide* cannot make you a theme writer, it can only help you along your way. In facing potential human annihilation at the light-speed circuits of robotic artificial intelligence, Morpheus knew their weakness, and he desperately had to share it with Neo: "I'm trying to free your mind, Neo. But I can only show you the door. You're the one that has to walk through it."

Theme:

"Examining what science has revealed about our evolving universe from the perspective of integral philosophy shows us how evolution is not random, accidental, or otherwise meaningless. On the contrary, its progressive advance reveals the presence of purpose—not an entirely preplanned or externally controlled type of purpose, but rather a creative generation of value that has been continually building upon itself for billions of years." —Steve McIntosh

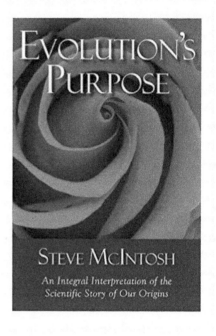

Technique: Throughout this *Field Guide*, I write many themes related to evolution, talk about universal processes that through evolution create our heritage and mark our journey along the evolutionary pathway toward greater complexity, self-organization, interconnectivity, and consciousness. Even this conclusion talks about the risks and rewards of technological evolution for the interpretive theme writer. I do this because I strongly believe that the topic of evolution is the most fundamental and far-reaching topic that we interpreters can ever present. Evolution spawns so many consequential themes that relate to all of our existential questions. It talks about spirituality, why we exist, how all things have come to be, where the universe is going, and the role of heritage in our lives. No topic bigger or more impacting exists. There is nothing that we interpret that does not relate to evolution. Evolution is debatable for some segments of society which adds to its relevance even for traditional, faith-based audiences. Although these audiences may be less inclined to debate the theme in any rational sense. For these reasons, I recommend that every interpreter learn about evolution, not just biological evolution, but evolution that has driven the development of the entire universe from the Big Bang forward across the four major spheres: cosmic, geologic, biological, and consciousness.

For a philosophical but fascinating treatment, see *Evolution's Purpose: An Integral Interpretation of the Scientific Story of Our Origins*. Also, for a more accessible read or viewing, see the *Journey of the Universe*, which is also a one-hour award-winning documentary. So many other sources can enrich your understanding.

Theme Notes

Theme Writing Exercise Responses

STATION 1 EXERCISES

1. Draw a line that links the communication type and its corresponding example.

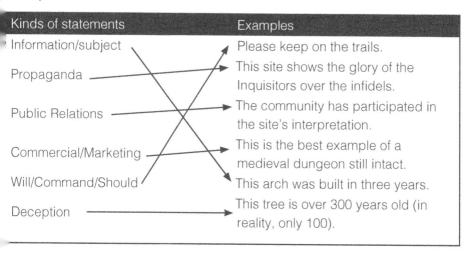

Kinds of statements	Examples
Information/subject	Please keep on the trails.
Propaganda	This site shows the glory of the Inquisitors over the infidels.
Public Relations	The community has participated in the site's interpretation.
Commercial/Marketing	This is the best example of a medieval dungeon still intact.
Will/Command/Should	This arch was built in three years.
Deception	This tree is over 300 years old (in reality, only 100).

2. Mark the following objectives most related to interpretation and justify your answer.

Objective	Related?	Why?
Students will be able to name the five bird species most commonly seen in this refuge.		*Memorization is not a goal of interpretation.*
Visitors will contribute to a fund that conserves the site's heritage values.	X	*Interpretation motivates people to protect a place for which they now feel deeper appreciation.*
Visitors will record "very satisfied" as the average response on a visitor satisfaction survey.		*Could be just entertainment.*
Visitors will develop a deeper appreciation for why the site's heritage is so important to the community's identity.	X	*Deeper appreciation is almost always a goal of interpretation.*
Visitors will be able to explain why parasites are such an important part of ecosystem function.	X	*Understanding in this context implies deeper appreciation, not just fact acquisition, but is audience dependent.*
Visitors will choose the site as the most entertaining recreational option within the community for Friday nights during the summer season.		*This is about recreation, not necessarily about thought provocation.*
Visitors will not step beyond the protective railing at the crater's edge.		*This is an enforcement objective.*
Visitor restaurant purchases will increase 5 percent annually from the 2018 baseline.		*This is a commercial objective that may have nothing to do with interpretation.*
Students will join the volunteer conservation corps at 10 percent annually from 2018 at the heritage site.	X	*Presumably only motivated students interested in the heritage would join.*
Retired population will indicate an increase in heritage pride after visiting the site.	X	*Pride is an emotional outcome of heritage interpretation.*

STATION 2 EXERCISE

Fill in the table below with the appropriate item from the list.

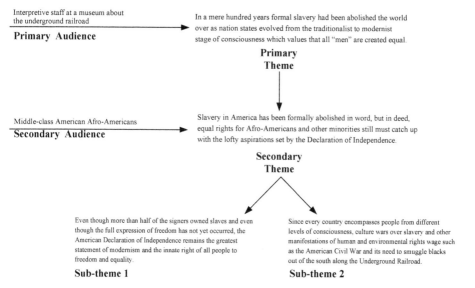

Interpretive staff at a museum about
the underground railroad

Primary Audience

In a mere hundred years formal slavery had been abolished the world
over as nation states evolved from the traditionalist to modernist
stage of consciousness which values that all "men" are created equal.

**Primary
Theme**

Middle-class American Afro-Americans

Secondary Audience

Slavery in America has been formally abolished in word, but in deed,
equal rights for Afro-Americans and other minorities still must catch up
with the lofty aspirations set by the Declaration of Independence.

**Secondary
Theme**

Even though more than half of the signers owned slaves and even
though the full expression of freedom has not yet occurred, the
American Declaration of Independence remains the greatest
statement of modernism and the innate right of all people to
freedom and equality.

Sub-theme 1

Since every country encompasses people from different
levels of consciousness, culture wars over slavery and other
manifestations of human and environmental rights wage such
as the American Civil War and its need to smuggle blacks
out of the south along the Underground Railroad.

Sub-theme 2

STATION 3 EXERCISE

Identify big and small ideas and justify your choice.

Idea	Size	Why?
Continuous war for centuries precipitated union in Europe.	B	*This may be the best example of regional block formation around the world among neighboring countries. The idea of the European Union is meant to stop centuries-old slaughter among neighbors.*
Big countries co-exist with small countries in Europe.	S	*This is a fact that offers no insight.*
Supra-national self-identity in the European Union generates more advanced ethical values.	B	*The implication is that a broader self-identity allows peoples to transcend the concept of the nation-state, which has implications for the development of other parts of the world.*
Several common languages bind the many countries of the European Union.	S	*An interesting fact without greater merit, argument, or provocative thought.*
People simultaneously act with a sense of national identity as well as European identity and this is not only acceptable but promoted across the continent.	B	*One could argue this is just a fact, but it also points to the nature of self-identity, no doubt disputed in different parts of Europe and tested by challenges such as Brexit and nationalist governments.*
There are almost as many countries in Europe (51) as there are in Africa (55).	S	*Most likely a historical coincidence.*

STATION 4 EXERCISE

Big Idea Test.

Check each criterion that applies to each proposed Big Idea; you may put a question mark when it is not possible to determine. This test presupposes that the statement has already been determined to be an interpretive statement.

Big Idea	Complete	Exciting	Logical	Revelatory	Clear	Universal
People believe their creation myths to help them understand their place in the world.	X	X	X	X	X	X
Human-produced greenhouse gases speed up climate change way beyond our ability to adapt to it.	X	?	X		X	X
Iguazu National Park is a World Heritage bi-national park.	X		X		X	
Popular super heroes symbolize human psychological archetypes.	X	?	?	X		X
Democracy is more a measure of social capital.			?	?		X
"The universe is made of stories, not atoms." —Muriel Rukeyser	X	X	?	X	?	X
"The most important scientific revolutions all include, as their only common feature, the dethronement of human arrogance from one pedestal after another of previous convictions about our centrality in the cosmos." —Stephen Jay Gould	X	X	X	X	X	X

STATION 5 EXERCISES

1. Weak vs. Strong Theme Practice

Theme	Strong or Weak	Why?
Since even small isolated plots of Lower Rio Grande Valley chaparral serve birds in the migratory flyway, habitat defragmentation can begin with backyards, unlike traditional conservation that begins with large blocks of habitat.	S	*Insightful and counter-intuitive understanding of conservation typically focused on large blocks.*
Adios to the heritage.	W	*What?*
The World Birding Center sites are portals to the rich birding matrix of the Lower Rio Grande Valley.	W	*Too much figurative language signifying nothing.*
Conservationists and ranchers both share a love for the same land in south Texas; their traditional mutual animosity is a leftover from 20th-century thinking.	S	*Points out an interesting irony that may have universal relevance.*
The Pueblo Culture Center traces the culture of the Pueblo Peoples.	W	*Simple fact*
The diversity and contrast of landscapes around the Middle Rio Grande Valley make it an interesting place.	W	*Marketing message.*
Hot summer days in Madrid.	W	*Not even a sentence.*
The destruction began here at Jamestown.	W	*Doesn't say anything.*
Protect the wildlife of Ashton Lagoon!	W	*Not a theme at all.*
Draining the lagoon of its water damages the ecosystem.	W	*Kind of obvious.*
Though hardening of the Rio Grande river channel has ended natural periodic flooding of riparian habitats, humans have inadvertently recreated this natural function with its acequia system.	S	*Interesting insight. The Acequia system is an irrigation and water channeling system inherited from the Pueblo people.*
The autonomous power of traditional wildlife refuge managers has empowered the public around Valle de Oro National Wildlife Refuge to participate in its management.	W	*It doesn't say how or why, which is the most important part.*
Artificial wetlands in Lower Rio Grande Valley eventually become real wetlands when water flow is restored from the Rio Grande.	S	*Interesting argument, not immediately apparent to most people. Could be stronger if universalized.*
Birds and butterflies both fly through the Greek islands.	W	*Duh.*
The Caribbean is a major byway not just for birds, but for people as well.	W	*Pointing to what could be an insight without stating what that insight is.*
The PUP Global Heritage Consortium has many interesting partners.	W	*Simple boring fact about an otherwise fascinating topic.*
Different people with different perspectives interpret the same events through completely different eyes, such as Hurricane Harvey, which could be God's punishment, a random event, or an effect of increasing Climate Chaos.	S	*Casts light on the nature of worldviews.*

2. Fill in the table with yes or no or an argument why you cannot definitively answer either way.

Questions/Themes	Since a single evolutionary force creates all heritage, the only difference between natural and cultural heritage are university departments that study them.	God is the universal force that drives all evolution of heritage.	Every culture in history has had a static worldview after world creation until modern science.
Is the theme interpretive rather than some other statement?	*Yes*	*Maybe not if this is considered marketing.*	*Maybe, though it is a straight fact, perhaps not hard to verify.*
Does it provoke rather than just provide easily verifiable information?	*Yes*	*Yes, but depends on the audience.*	*Maybe, but depends on the audience.*
Does it avoid postponing the Big Idea?	*No*	*No*	*No*
Does it excite you? Do you want to know more?	*Yes*	*No, but depends on the audience.*	*Maybe, depending on audience.*
Can you imagine an entire program based on this theme?	*Maybe*	*Yes*	*Yes*
Does it pass the test?	*Yes*	*No*	*No*

STATION 6 EXERCISE

Convert the Big Idea into a strong interpretive theme.

Big Idea	Strong Interpretive Theme
Geologically, Native Americans are as much visitors as Europeans are.	*On a human time scale, 14,000 years or so of First Nation habitation in the Americas may sound like eternity, but on a geological or species time scale, such habitation is very recent contrasted with hominid evolution in Africa.*
On the map, Australia is no more down under than Russia.	*As Earth hurdles through space, humans use arbitrary and relative parameters to orient themselves such as north-south, up-down, and us-them.*
Growth is the measure of both macroeconomic progress and doom.	*Although global leaders believe economic growth to be the solution to all social problems, that same growth will smack into limits that results, ironically, in economic collapse.*
The goal is to die in the largest, most encompassing paradigm/worldview possible.	*As people mature, they shed older, more limited paradigms and grow into larger ones that explain more about the world.*
Name your own.	*Write your own.*

STATION 7 EXERCISES

Exercise 1: Place the following components from the interpretive framework of Chagres National Park in Panama into the following framework table.

Dense forest harvests clouds and rain, pumping them along the Chagres River

Dispersion	Water cycle (Foehm Effect)	Solar energy maintains civilization	Conquest and rebirth	Succession and migration	Cultural assimilation

Interoceanic Communication: The Chagres River communicates between oceans via commerce, cultures, and even genes.

Intersection of Biodiversity *A well conserved forest is genetically strengthened and strengthens other forests through direct connectivity.*	**Water Passage** *Chagres National Park does not only contribute 40 percent of the water for the Panama Canal and for the consumption of 1.7 million people, but also contributes to Panama's national image.*	**From the Ancient Road to the Modern Royal Road** *The same Camino Real (Royal Road) that connected interoceanic and prehispanic commerce became the principal route for the Spanish colonization that extracted gold from the New World and sent it to the Old, thus paving the way for rural and urban settlement in the center of Panama.*	**Safe Distance** *Although Western culture impacted the heritage of many indigenous people, the Emberá have conserved their heritage over time, despite being so close to Western culture.*

Harpy Eagle	Chagres River	Lowest cloud forest in Central America	Panama Canal	Royal Road	Emberá Drúa Village

Exercise 2: Integrate Themes into Higher-Level Themes

Universal Themes	Throwing Salt on the Sacred Wound		Glaciations and Biodiversity	
	Commerce along the Salt Route unleashed a wave of desecration of indigenous territory.		*The milennial expansion and retrocession of glaciers in El Cocuy National Park created refuges that permit speciation along altitudinal gradients.*	
Local Themes	**The Salt Route**	**Desecration**	**Glacial Masses**	**Biodiversity and Endemism**
	Commercial traffic along the Salt Route, whether indigenous or Spanish, drove the cultural and territorial domination of El Cocuy and its surroundings.	Despite the fact that the Spanish brought the Holy Cross to extend their religion over the indigenous cosmovision, in reality, they desecrated their land.	Although the snowcap mountains of Güicán, Cocuy and Chita have one of the most extensive glacial masses north of the equator, the peaks that were once covered in ice, one by one, are melting.	Given the altitudinal gradient that cuts across extensive forests and paramos and the resulting abundance of habitat, El Cocuy National Park is the heart of high levels of biodiversity and endemism, such as the *(Frailejón Epeletia cleffi)* and collard lizard *(Stenocercus lache)*.

Verbs for Stronger Themes and More Engaging Commentaries

The following list comes from Sam's 2013 book, *Interpretation: Making a Difference on Purpose*. He says, "I've tried to select verbs that are simple, common, and understandable by most native-English-speaking adults. I've tried to include mainly verbs that describe easily imagined/easily visualized actions or which make interesting sounds. Notice how many interesting verbs begin with the letter s."

A
abandon abduct abhor
abort absorb abuse
accelerate accept
accompany account ache
act activate adapt adhere
adjust admire adorn
advance aerate affect
aggravate aggregate
agitate agonize aid ail
aim alarm alert align
allure alternate amass
amaze amble ambush
amplify amputate amuse
analyze anchor anger
angle anguish annihilate
annoy appeal appear
append applaud apply
apprehend arch argue
arise arm arouse arrest
arrive ascend asphyxiate
assassinate assault
astound attach attack
avalanche avenge awe
axe

B
babble baby back backfire
backhand backlash
backslide badger bag bail
bake balk balloon band
bar bare barge bark barrel
barricade bat bate bathe
batter battle beam bear
beat beckon befuddle
beg behead belch belt
bend bewitch bind bisect
bite blanket blare blast
blaze bleach bleed blend
blister bloom blossom blur

blurt blush bluster board
bob bog (down) boggle
bolt bombard bond bore
bother bounce bow braid
branch brave break breath
breathe breeze brew
brighten bristle broadside
broil browse bruise bubble
buckle bud budge bully
bum bump bunch bundle
bungle buoy (up) burden
burn burnish burp burrow
burst bury bustle butcher
butt buzz bypass

C
cache cackle cage calm
camouflage cannibalize
canvass cap capsize
captivate capture caress
carpet cart carve cascade
cast catalogue catapult
catch cave (in) cease
celebrate cement center
chafe channel chap char
charge charm chart chase
cheapen cheat check
cheer cherish chill chime
chip chisel choke chop
christen chronicle chuck
chug churn circle clack
clamber clamor clamp
clang clash clasp claw
cleanse clear cleave
clench click climax climb
clinch cling clink clip
cloak clobber clock clog
clothe cloud clown club
cluster clutch clutter
coast coat coerce coil

collapse collar comb
combat combust comfort
compact compress
conceal concoct condemn
condense confine congeal
connect conquer console
conspire constrain
constrict consume contrast
converge convulse cool
cope copulate corner
corral corrode couple
court cover cower crack
(down) crackle cradle craft
cram crane crank crash
crave crawl creak crease
creep cremate crest cringe
crinkle cripple crisscross
croak crook croon cross
crossbreed crouch crow
crowd crown crucify cruise
crumble crumple crunch
crush crust cry crystallize
cuddle cup curb curl curve
cushion cuss cut cycle

D
dab dabble dam dampen
dance dangle dare darken
dart dash daub dawn
daze dazzle deaden
deafen decapitate decay
decelerate decimate
decorate decoy deepen
defecate defend deflate
deflect deflower defoliate
deforest deform defy
degenerate degrade
demand demolish
demonstrate den dent
denude deodorize depict

deplete deposit deprive derail descend desert desiccate despoil destroy detach detect detonate detour devastate devour dice die dig digest dim dip dirty disable disarm discover disengage disentangle disintegrate dislodge dismember dismount disperse displace disrobe dissect dissolve disturb dive divide dodge dog dominate doodle doom dot double douse dovetail doze drag drain dramatize drape dream dredge drench dribble drift drill drink drip drive drizzle drone drool droop drop drown drum dry dry-run duck duel dull dump dunk dust dwarf dwindle dye

E

ease eat eavesdrop echo eclipse edge (away) eject eke (out) elate elbow electrify elevate elude emancipate embark embarrass embed embellish embody embrace embroil emerge emit empower empty enable enact enamor encase enchant enclose encompass encounter encroach endanger endow endure energize engage enhance enlarge enliven enrich enslave entangle enthuse entomb entrap entrench entwine envelop envision equip eradicate erase erode erupt escalate escape escort etch evacuate evade evaporate evict excavate excise excite exclude

excrete exhale exhaust exhilarate exhume expand expel expire explode exploit explore expose exterminate extract exude eye eyeball

F

fabricate face fade fail fake fall fan fancy fantasize farm fascinate fashion fasten father fatigue favor fear feast feature feed feel feign fell fend (off, for) ferret (out) ferry fertilize fester fetch fetter feud fight file fill filter find finesse finger fire fish fit fix fizz fizzle flake flame flank flare (up) flash flatten flaunt flavor flee flex flicker flinch fling flip flirt float flock flog flood floor flop flounder flourish flow flower fluff flush flutter fly foam focus fog foil fold fondle fool (with, around) forage forbear force foresee foretell forge fork form fortify fossilize fracture frame frazzle free freeload freeze freshen frighten frolic frost froth frown fruit fudge fuel fumble fume funnel fuse fuss

G

gab gabble gaff gag gallop gamble (on) gape garble gas gash gasp gather gauge gawk gaze gel generate germinate gesture giggle girdle glance glare glaze gleam glide glimmer glisten glitter glow glue glut gnarl gnash goad gobble goof gore gorge gouge grab grapple grasp grate gratify

gravitate graze grease greet grieve grill grin grind grip gripe grit groan groom groove grope group growl grub grumble grunt guard guide gulp gum (up) gurgle gush gut guzzle gyrate

H

hack haggle halt halve hammer hamper hand handcuff handle hang harbor harden harm harmonize harness harp hassle hatch hate haul haunt hawk hazard haze head heal heap heat heave heckle hedge heighten herd hew (out) hiss hit hitch hobble hog hogtie hoist hollow (out) hone hood hoof hook hoot hop horrify horse (around) hose hound house hover howl huddle hug hum humidify humiliate hunger (for) hunt hurdle hurl hurt hush hustle hydrate hydroplane hypnotize

I

ice ignite illuminate image imagine imbue imitate immerse immigrate immobilize impair impale impede implant implode implore imprint imprison improvise inbreed incapacitate incarcerate inch incite incubate induce indulge inebriate infect inflame inflate inflict infuriate infuse ingest inhale inhibit inject injure ink inlay inoculate inscribe insert inspect install instill insulate intensify interact interbreed intercept interfere interfold interlace interlink interlock interplay interrupt intersperse

intertwine interweave
intoxicate intrude inundate
invade invert investigate
invigorate ionize irrigate
irritate isolate itch

J

jab jabber jack jacket
jackknife jail jam jangle jar
jaunt jaw jeer jell jerk jest
jet jiggle jimmy jingle jitter
jog join jolt jostle jot (down)
journey juggle jumble jump
junk jut (out) juxtapose

K

kayak kick kill kink kiss
knead knee kneel knife knit
knock knot knuckle (down,
under)

L

label labor lace lacerate
ladle lag lance land lap
lash (out) lasso latch lather
laugh launch layer leach
lead leak lean leap lecture
leer leg (out) level liberate
lie lift light limp line linger
lip litter liven load lob lock
lodge log long (for) loom
loop loosen lounge love
lower lubricate lug lull
lumber lump lunge lurch
lure lurk

M

madden magnify maim
mangle map mar march
marinate mark (up) marry
martyr marvel mash mask
masquerade massacre
massage master mate
mature maul meander
meet meld mellow melt
mend merge mesh
mesmerize migrate milk
mill (around) mime mimic
mince mingle miniaturize
moan mob mock model

moisten mold molest molt
monkey (with, around)
mop (up) mother motion
motor mottle mount mourn
mouth move mow muck
(around) muddle muffle
mug mulch mumble
munch murder murmur
muscle mush mushroom
muster mute mutilate
mutter muzzle mystify

N

nab nag nail nap narrow
navigate near needle nest
nestle net nibble nip nod
nose notice nourish nudge
numb number nurse
nurture nuzzle

O

oar obscure obstruct
offend oil ooze open
operate oppose orbit
originate ornament
orphan oscillate ostracize
oust outclass outcrop
outdistance outdo
outfit outgrow outlive
outmaneuver outmatch
outrage outreach outrun
outshine outsmart outsoar
outspeak outspread
outstay outstretch
outstrip outtalk outwear
outweigh outwit outwork
overact overcome
overcrowd overdo
overdress overexpose
overflow overhang
overhear overindulge
overlap overlay overload
overlook overnight
overpower overproduce
overreact overrun oversee
overshadow overshoot
oversleep overtake overtax
overthrow overturn overuse
overwhelm overwork

P

pace pacify pack package
pad paddle pain paint
pair pale palm pamper
pan panhandle panic pant
pantomime parade parallel
paralyze parch pare park
part partition party paste
pat patch patrol patter
pause pave pawn peak
peck pedal peddle peel
peep peer peg pellet
pelt pen pencil penetrate
pepper perch percolate
perforate perform perfume
perish perk (up) permeate
persevere persist personify
perspire perturb peruse
pervade pester pet petrify
pickle picture piddle
pierce piggyback pile pilfer
pillage pilot pin pinch pine
pioneer pipe pirate pitch
pivot place plague plant
plaster plate platoon play
plead please plot plow
pluck plug plummet plump
(up, out) plunder plunge
plunk poach pocket
point poise poison polish
pollute pommel ponder
pool pop pore portage
portion pose position
post pounce pound pour
powder power powwow
pray preach preen press
pressure prevail prey
prime prize probe prod
project prop (up) propel
protect protrude prowl
prune pry pucker puff pull
pulsate pulverize pummel
pump punch punish purge
purify purr push pussyfoot
putrefy puzzle

Q

quack quadruple quaff
quake quarantine quarrel
quarry quarter quash

quaver quell quench
quibble quicken quiet
quintuple quip quit quiver
quiz

R

race rack radiate raft rage
raid rail rain raise rake
rally ram ramble rampage
ramrod ranch rankle
ransack rant rap rape rasp
rat rattle ravage rave ravel
ravish razz react ream
reap rebel rebound rebuke
recede recline recoil
recover recuperate reduce
reek reel reflect reforest
refresh refuel regain
regenerate regret regulate
regurgitate rehabilitate
rehash rehearse reign
reinforce rejuvenate relax
release relent relieve
relinquish relish remain
remedy remodel remove
render renew renounce
renovate reopen repair
repeat repel replace
replenish replicate reply
report repress reprieve
reproach reproduce
repulse rescue research
resemble reshape reside
resist resonate respond
rest restore restrain restrict
resume resurrect retain
retake retaliate retard
retire retort retouch retrace
retract retreat retrieve
return reunite revamp
reveal revel reverberate
reverse revive revolt
revolve reward rework
rhyme rib ribbon ricochet
rid riddle ride ridge
ridicule riffle rifle rift rig
right rim ring rinse riot
rip ripen ripple rise risk
rival rivet roam roar roast
rob robe rock rocket roll

roller-coaster romance
romanticize romp room
roost root rope rot rotate
round rouse rout rove
row rub (down) ruffle ruin
rumble rummage run
rupture rush rust rustle rut

S

sabotage sack sacrifice
safeguard sag sail salivate
salt salvage sample
sand sandbag sandblast
sandwich sanitize sap sass
satiate satisfy saturate
saunter sauté save savor
saw scaffold scald scale
scalp scamper scan scar
scare scarf scathe scatter
scavenge scent school
scintillate scoff scold
scoop scorch scorn scour
scout scowl scrabble
scram scramble scrap
scrape scratch scrawl
scream screech screen
screw scribble scribe
scrimp script scroll scrub
scrunch scrutinize scuff
scuffle sculpt sculpture
scurry scuttle seal seam
sear search season seat
seclude second-guess
secrete section secure
sedate seduce seed seek
seep seethe segment
segregate seize send
sense sensitize separate
serenade serpentine serve
set settle sever shackle
shade shadow shake
shampoo shape sharpen
shatter shave shear shed
sheer shell shelter shelve
shepherd shield shift shim
shimmer shin shine shingle
shinny ship shiver shock
shoot shore (up) short-
circuit shorten shoulder
shout shove shovel show

shower shred shriek shrill
shrink shrivel shroud shrug
shuck shudder shuffle shun
shush shut (up) shuttle
shy (away) sicken sideline
sideslip sidestep sidetrack
sift sigh sight sign signal
silence simmer simulate sin
sing singe sink sip siphon
sire sit situate size (up)
sizzle skate skeletonize
sketch skew skewer ski
skid skim skin skip skirmish
skirt skitter skunk sky
slacken slam slant slap
slash slaughter slay sled
sledge sleep (on, off)
sleigh slice slick(en) slide
slime sling slip slit slither
slobber slog slop slope
slosh slouch slough slow
slug slum slump slur slurp
smack smart smash smear
smell smile smirk smoke
smooth smooth talk smothe
smudge snack snag
snake snap snare snarl
snatch sneak sneer sneeze
snicker sniff sniffle snip
snitch snoop snooze snore
snorkel snort snow snowba
snowshoe snuff (out)
snuggle soak (up) soapbo)
soar sob sober (up) sock
sod soft-pedal soften soil
soldier solidify soot soothe
sop sound sour souse
sow space spade span
spank spar spare spark
sparkle spatter spawn
spear speckle speed spell
spellbind spend spew
spice (up) spike spill spin
spindle spiral spit splash
splice splint split splotch
spoil sponge spoof spoon
spoon-feed spot spout
sprawl spray spread sprin(
springboard sprinkle sprou
spruce (up) spume spur

spurt sputter spy squabble
squall squash squat
squawk squeak squeal
squeeze squelch squint
squirrel (around) squirm
squirt squish stab stabilize
stack stage stagger stain
stake stalk stall stammer
stamp stampede stand
stare starve stash station
stay steal steam steep
steepen steer stench step
(up) sterilize stew stick stiff
stiffen stifle still stimulate
sting stink (up) stir (up)
stitch stoke stomach
stomp stone stonewall
stoop storm stow straddle
straggle straighten strain
strand strap stray streak
stream strengthen stress
stretch strew stride strike
string strip stroke stroll
strong-arm struggle strut
stub study stuff stumble
stump stun stunt stupefy
stutter stutter-step
stymie subdivide subdue
submarine submerge
submerse submit (to)
subside subvert succumb
suck sucker suckle suffer
suffocate sugarcoat sulk
summer summon sun
supercharge superimpose
supply support suppress
surf surface surge
surmount surpass surprise
surrender surround survey
survive suspect suspend
sustain suture swab
swagger swallow swamp
swap swarm swash swat
sway swear sweat sweep
sweeten swell swelter
swerve swill swim swindle
swing swipe swirl swish
switch swivel swoop
symbolize sympathize
systemize

T

tack tackle tag tail tailor
take tally tame tamp
tamper (with) tan tangle
tantalize tap tape taper
target tarnish taste tatter
tattle tattoo taunt tax taxi
teach team (up) tear tear
(up) [cry] tease teem
teeter telegraph tell
temper tempt tense (up)
tent terminate terrace
terrify terrorize test testify
tether texture thatch thaw
thicken thin think thirst
thrash thread threaten
thrill thrive throb throttle
throw thrust thud thumb
thump thunder thwart tick
tickle tie tighten till tilt time
ting tinge tingle tinker tint
tip tiptoe tire titillate toast
toboggan toddle toggle
toil tolerate tomahawk
tone (up, down) tongue
tool toot top topple torch
torment torpedo torture
toss tote totter touch tour
tow towel tower toy trace
track traffic trail train
tramp trample transcend
transfer transform transmit
transplant transport trap
trash travel traverse tread
treat tree trek tremble
trench trespass trick trickle
trigger trill trim trip triple
trisect triumph trouble
trounce trowel truck trudge
trumpet truncate tuck
tug tumble tune (up, out)
tunnel turn tutor twang
tweet twiddle twine twinge
twinkle twirl twist twitch

U

unarm unbalance unbind
unbolt unbox unbuckle
unclench unclothe uncoil
uncork uncouple uncover

uncross undercut underdo
underdress underfeed
undergo underlay
undermine underscore
undress undulate unearth
unfasten unfold unfurl
unharness unhinge unhitch
unhook unify unite unlace
unlatch unleash unlink
unload unlock unmask
unmuffle unmuzzle
unnerve unpack unpin
unravel unroll unscramble
unscrew unseat unsettle
unsnap unsnarl unstick
unstrap unstring untangle
unthread untie untwist
unveil unwind unwrap
upraise uproot upset
upstage upturn urge
urinate usher usurp utter

V

vacate vaccinate vacillate
validate vandalize vanish
vanquish vaporize varnish
vault veer vegetate veil
vent ventilate venture (in,
into) verbalize verify veto
vex vibrate view vindicate
violate visit visualize
vitalize vivify vocalize
voice void vomit vote vow
voyage vulgarize

W

wad waddle wade waffle
wag wager waggle wail
wait waken wale walk
wallop wallow wander
wane want war warble
ward (off) warm warn
warp wash watch water
wave wax weaken wean
wear (in, on, out) weasel
(out) weather weave
wedge weed weep weigh
weld well (up, forth)
welt wet whack whap
wheel wheeze whet whiff

whimper whine whinny
whip whir whirl whish whisk
whisper whistle whitewash
whittle whiz whoop widen
widow wield wiggle
wigwag wile (away) will
wilt win wince winch wind
wing wink winter winterize
wipe wire witch withdraw
wither withhold witness
wobble wolf wonder woo
word work worm worry
wow wrack wrangle wrap
wreathe wreck wrench
wrest wrestle wriggle wring
wrinkle write wrong

X
x-ray

Y
yak yammer yank yap yard
yarn yawn yearn yellow
yelp yen yield yip yodel

Z
zap zero (in) zigzag zing
zip zone zonk (out) zoom

Field Inventory of Strong Themes in this *Field Guide*

This inventory showcases the following strong themes in this *Field Guide*. Weak themes such as those designed to illustrate poor technique have been omitted. All themes by Jon Kohl unless otherwise cited.

My culture conditions me to experience myself as separate from everyone and everything else—indeed, I am a single self-aware being floating untethered in space; but strong interpretive themes can re-connect our separate selves to higher truths about humanity and Nature so that we may sew ourselves back into the fabric of the evolving universe.
Trailhead
Theme Spotlight: Theme of Themes

As humanity faces a civilization-sized threat in climate change caused by its relationship with a finite planet, technological answers such as switching fossil fuels for alternative sources, will only remedy, not solve, the underlying problem.
Station 1
Theme Spotlight: Strong vs. Weak Themes

"The illiterate of the 21st century will not be those who cannot read or write, but those who cannot learn, unlearn, and relearn." —Alvin Toffler
Station 1
Theme Spotlight: Message vs. Theme

Two hundred million years of dinosaurian dominance on Earth did not influence naming of geological time periods, while human building and cropping for mere thousands may result in the naming of the Anthropocene Epoch.
Station 2
Example of a primary theme

Secondary theme for children: Dinosaurs lived a very long time and didn't change the earth. People have been here for a much shorter time. Yet we have changed the oceans, skies, and land. (fifth-grade level, 10- to 11-year-olds)

Secondary theme for conservationists: Changing geological time periods have been named in part for mass extinctions caused by geological and climatic factors; now, for the first time, the current mass extinction is caused by a biological factor: the human species.

Secondary theme for birders: The ancestors of birds flew and jumped with other dinosaurs for millions of years during which the geological time period did not change; now after mere millennia of human building and cropping, and the extinction of numerous charismatic bird species, the name may change to the Anthropocene Epoch.

Station 2
Examples of secondary themes based on the above primary theme

"Valle de Oro extends the gradient of engaging activities that traditional refuges offer right up to the doorstep of every urban dweller, no matter their prior experience with wildlife or its protection."

Station 2
Valle de Oro National Wildlife Refuge Interpretive Framework
Agency mission-based primary theme

"Eco-political challenges drive local residents to seek higher aspirations for their community and habitat."

"Overcoming adversity drives the evolution of consciousness and achievement of greater human aspirations."

"As people fulfill many of their more basic human needs, their consciousness expands, and they fight for wider social and environmental needs."

"Difficult socio-economic and environmental conditions require that people develop a pioneering attitude to persevere and prosper."

Station 2
Theme Spotlight: Themes vs. Sub-Themes
Ashton Lagoon Interpretive Framework

Even though more than half of the signers owned slaves and even though the full expression of freedom had not yet occurred, the American *Declaration of Independence* remains the greatest statement of the innate right of all people to freedom and equality.

Slavery in America has been formally abolished in word, but in deed, equal rights for African-Americans and other minorities still must catch up with the lofty aspirations set by the *Declaration of Independence.*

Since every country includes people with varying levels of consciousness, culture wars over slavery and other manifestations of human and environmental rights wage such as the American Civil War and its need to smuggle blacks out of the south along the Underground Railroad.

In a mere hundred years formal slavery had been abolished the world over as nation states evolved from traditional to modern consciousness which values that all "men" are created equal.
Station 2 exercise

Sex between people, as well as the spiritual drive to improve the world, are examples of the same creative impulse that has made the universe more complex and mysterious since its beginning: The Big Bang.
Station 3
Theme Spotlight: Big Idea vs. Interpretive Theme

The only distinction between World Heritage and everything else are the meanings that we assign.
Station 3
Theme Spotlight: Theme Writing vs. Theme Development

Despite the crowds that throng the valley floor, Yosemite is a 'de-peopled' landscape."
–Ann Lundberg

We often think of wilderness as a geographical place, but time is also a wilderness."
–Ann Lundberg
Station 3
Theme Spotlight: Themes Should Present an Argument

Due to human modification of planetary systems, the time may be right to rename our current geological epoch as the Anthropocene.
Station 3
Theme Spotlight: Theme = Object + Big Idea

We do not see things as they are; we see things as we are." —The Talmud

We become just by performing just actions, temperate by performing temperate actions, brave by performing brave actions." —Aristotle

The world we have created is a product of our thinking; it cannot change without changing our thinking." —Albert Einstein

Material abundance without character is the path of destruction." —Thomas Jefferson

There is no greater agony than bearing an untold story inside you." —Maya Angelou

"All major cultural realignments and shifts in worldview carry great confusion, lack of personal integration, and the usual fringe elements. This was true with the Reformation and the Enlightenment, and it is true with our current cultural crises."
—Mark Woodhouse
Station 4
Big Ideas in the form of aphorism, sayings, proverbs, with universal value.

The meaning of artifacts depends on who owns them and who tells their story. Enduring civilizations have stable and productive economies that allow for the accumulation of wealth.

Physical geography influences the characteristics and success or decline of civilizations. The way material behaves depends on how its atoms are arranged.

Correlation in data is not the same as causation in data.
—All from *Learning That Lasts*
Station 4
Additional Big Ideas

The collapse of human civilizations is not a history of slowly degrading ability to provide basic services, but a long ignorance of society's decline by its leaders.
Station 4
Theme Spotlight: Connecting Unlike Points to Cast New Light

A graveyard, much more than a respectable space to dispose of the deceased, concentrates spiritual meaning into a sacred, inhabited place.

A drought doesn't just alter plant and animal communities, but may even alter the very identity of the place itself.

The remote control represents the transformation of the American living room by the couch-centered leisure industry into middle-class society's final resting place.

When organisms face challenges, evolution selects for successful solutions that do not exclude other possible solutions as well, such as humpback whales that communicate over thousands of kilometers with audible songs rather than, for instance, chemical signals or telepathy.

Different minerals, like diamonds, emerge from the evolving complexity of Earth, born of space dust and energy.

Despite that geology is the study of rocks, the current geological period may be renamed based on human not geologic activity.

Technological development has been largely a story of extending and replacing human physical and cognitive capacities to increase productivity, from the simplest functions of hands to perhaps the most advanced functions of the self-reflecting mind.
Station 4
Results of different Big Idea approaches

Behind the artistic beauty of the colonial architecture of Antigua, Guatemala lurks the conquistadors' hidden plan to dominate people's own artistic expression and religious customs.
Station 4
Theme Spotlight: A Revelation-Irony Theme

It is actually more cost effective for birds to migrate thousands of kilometers twice a year than figure out how to survive in winter.
Station 4
Qualities of Big Ideas

'If the rate of expansion one second after the Big Bang had been smaller by even one part in a hundred thousand million million, the universe would have recollapsed before it ever reached its present size." —Stephen Hawking

Humans can access the ground of being, that intangible field out of which tangible material arises now, before the Big Bang, and possibly forever.

People may be literally connected to each other beyond the boundaries of birth and death.
Station 4
Facts that serve as provocative themes

The probability of a shift in worldview is directly proportional to the extent we acknowledge that we are not dealing with isolated trends." —Mark Woodhouse

Reality divided by reason always leaves a remainder." —Daniel Kim

After the Big Bang, every distinction is arbitrary. —Buckminster Fuller (Allegedly)

To optimize the whole, we must sub-optimize the parts." —W. Edward Deming

"We can see how every truth and every error, each a thought of someone's mind, clothes itself with societies, houses, cities, language, ceremonies, newspapers."
—Ralph Waldo Emerson
Station 4
Clear but not necessarily quickly understood

As government or ways of governing change, often it is necessary to destroy the previous form and sometimes those who promote the change as well.

All ecosystems eventually experience some natural "disaster" or violent change (forest fires, earthquakes, hurricanes) that rapidly releases their energy (for example, stored as trees) which then is reused in a new phase of growth and evolution.

Colonization of new lands speeds up as the colonizers learn more about those new lands.

Colonization of new lands speeds up as the colonizers learn more about those new lands, such as through the writings and adventures of Captain John Smith.

Because human ability to adapt is based on our innovative technological mind rather than our physical bodies, our species has colonized almost all habitats on planet Earth.

The evolution of cultural memes rather than biological genes has allowed humans to rapidly adapt to nearly all habitats on planet Earth.
Station 4
Universalized themes

Fifteenth- and sixteenth-century military coastal forts like Fort Jesus in Mombasa, Kenya, protected, consolidated, and coordinated East African trade and sea routes to the Far East for the dominant foreign powers, hence the control of what would have remained in the chaos of piracy and conflict.

There is no such thing as natural disasters, only natural phenomena, such as Hurricanes Harvey, Florence, and María, which damage human systems built with development decisions that do not prioritize resilience.
Station 4
Add local examples if you want themes with universal value

People believe their creation myths to help them understand their place in the world.

Human-produced greenhouse gases speed up climate change way beyond our ability to adapt to it.

"The most important scientific revolutions all include, as their only common feature, the dethronement of human arrogance from one pedestal after another of previous convictions about our centrality in the cosmos." —Stephen Jay Gould

Station 4 exercise

Four and a half billion years of Earth's deep time have produced all the geological time periods until present; now scientists may rename the current epoch to the Anthropocene after mere millennia of human alteration.

Two hundred million years of dinosaurian dominance on Earth did not influence naming of geological time periods, while human building and cropping for mere thousands may result in the naming of the Anthropocene Epoch.

Until now the naming of Earth's geological time periods has relied exclusively on colossal churning, mixing, and solidifying of megatons of rocks over eons; the next time period however may be named solely for human civilization-building.

Station 5
Knockan Theory

"The invention of printing radically changed ways of thinking—not just how things are communicated, but what can be thought." —Derrick de Kerckhove

"[T]here is nothing more difficult to carry out, nor more doubtful of success, nor more dangerous to handle, than to initiate a new order of things. For the reformer has enemies in all those who profit by the old order, and only lukewarm defenders in all those who would profit by the new order." —Niccolò Machiavelli.

"Almost always the men who achieve these fundamental inventions of a new paradigm have been either very young or very new to the field whose paradigm they change." —Thomas Kuhn

"Throwing Salt on the Sacred Wound: Commerce along the Salt Route unleashed a wave of desecration of indigenous territory." —El Cocuy National Park Interpretive Framework

"Despite the fact that the Spanish brought the Holy Cross to extend their religion over the indigenous cosmovision, in reality, they desecrated their land." —El Cocuy National Park Interpretive Framework

"Fifteenth and Sixteenth Century global economic powers, like Portugal, Spain, and Oman battled to dominate the lifeblood trade routes of the high seas, yet their oceanic success depended ironically on land-bound forts." —Fort Jesus National Monument

"Mombasa's strategic location, critical for controlling the East African trade routes, attracted fierce competitors from distant Europe and Asia. Yet the violent and on-going clashes which led to Fort Jesus changing hands six times, ironically seeded a diverse and tolerant cultural mix of peoples living there today." —Fort Jesus National Monument

Many biologists believe that evolution refers only to biology, but in reality, evolution goes much beyond Darwin, beginning with the Big Bang.

"In recent centuries, the Flint Hills have suffered various displacements of its (non)human inhabitants, leaving behind fragmented communities, but enriching its overall natural and cultural diversity." —Flint Hills Discovery Center Interpretive Framework

"Migration and cultivation, traditionally guided by natural cycles, have been fragmented by modern transportation and production systems creating complex landscape mosaics." —Valle de Oro Interpretive Framework

Governments fight drug trafficking in Colombia where local farmers grow coca, while invisible and blameless consumers in distant lands drive the demand for cocaine.

"As far as the laws of mathematics refer to reality, they are not certain; and as far as they are certain, they do not refer to reality." —Albert Einstein

What distinguishes World Heritage Sites from other protected areas is the ease with which the Sites can tie together the heart of a person with the heart of humanity.
Station 5
Spicy ingredients

Raised with unconditional love in Skopje, Mother Theresa demonstrated that while the body must have food, water, air, and shelter to survive, only unconditional love can heal damages to the spirit, open doors closed by hate, and restore even the most indigent to dignity.
Station 5
Theme Spotlight: Transformative Themes Tap Existential Truths

Ants have innovated farming strategies (aphid herding and fungi cultivation) millennia before people "invented" their own farming systems.
Station 5
Theme Spotlight: Adding Human Condition to Non-Human Phenomena

"The health of a democratic society may be measured by the quality of functions performed by private citizens." —Alexis de Tocqueville

Long theme: "Our culture does not nourish that which is best or noblest in the human spirit. It does not cultivate vision, imagination, or aesthetic or spiritual sensitivity. It does not encourage gentleness, generosity, caring, or compassion. Increasingly in the late 20th Century, the economic-technocratic-statist worldview has become a monstrous destroyer of what is loving and life-affirming in the human soul." —Ron Miller

Station 5
Brevity

"For just as the Milky Way is the universe in the form of a flower, we are the universe in the form of a human. And every time we are drawn to look up in the night sky and reflect on the awesome beauty of the universe, we are actually the universe reflecting on itself." —Brian Swimme

Station 5
Theme Spotlight: Can a Theme Have More than One Sentence?

To date, Earth's geologic time periods have been named only for changing rocks. Now, the current period may be renamed for human activity.

Station 5
Readability

Although all geological periods to date have been defined based on geological change, our current epoch exhibits geologic change—such as Glacier National Park's melting glaciers—in cultural time.

By applying a remedy to one sore, you will provoke another: and that which removes the one ill symptom produces others, whereas the strengthening one part of the body weakens the rest." —Sir Thomas More, Utopia.

As the geology field gazed upon acts of humanity, it knew that it could no longer name its time periods for geological criteria alone.

Crowns throughout history always fight to retain their power even when the weary people demand a change.

The maritime discoverers sailed their cultural and urban models around the world.

The eyes see only what the mind is prepared to comprehend." —Henri Bergson.

Bullies are often people who are shy and can't make friends easily, so, as the theme of the movie 'A Bronx Tale' tells us, it is better to be feared if you can't be loved." —Philip Zimbardo

Station 5
Figurative language

"The one recurring theme in my writing, and in my life in general, is confusion. The fact that anytime you think you really know something, you're going to find out you're wrong—that is the rule. The moments where you think you have something figured out, those are the exceptions." —Conor Oberst

"You can never change things by fighting the existing reality. To change something, build a new model that makes the existing model obsolete." —F. Buckminster Fuller
Station 5
Generic "you"

Because primary forests bear few if any recognizable signs of humanity, people associate them with prehistory, a time once considered purer and closer to the divine.
Station 5
Clarity

From sea-bottom sediments to molecules that bounce in the sky, humans have scarred the entire planet surface, provoking the arrival of the Anthropocene.
Station 5
Strong verbs and nouns

Until now, scientists have named time periods based on changes in geology; now, they propose to rename the current epoch based on anthropology.
Station 5
Active voice

Though today we commonly associate globalization with virtual entities such as the Internet and worldwide banking, when globalization was born, arguably with the Portuguese discoverers in the 15th century, physical military fortifications such as Fort Jesus tied together their globalizing threads.

Fort Jesus in Mombasa defended Portuguese shipping lanes before the advent of canons rendered the fort obsolete.
Station 5
Generality v. universality

Earth's history has always earned its time-period names based on geological change; now, for the first time, scientists propose renaming the current epoch for human change.
Station 5
Power positions

Since even small isolated plots of Lower Rio Grande Valley chaparral serve birds in the migratory flyway, habitat defragmentation can begin with backyards, unlike traditional conservations that begins with large blocks of habitat.

Conservationists and ranchers both share a love for the same land in south Texas; their traditional mutual animosity is a leftover from 20th-century thinking.

Though hardening of the Rio Grande river channel has ended natural periodic flooding of riparian habitats, humans have inadvertently recreated this natural function with its acequia system.

Different people with different perspectives interpret the same events through completely different eyes, such as Hurricane Harvey, which could be God's punishment, a random event, or an effect of increasing Climate Chaos.
Station 5 exercise

On a human time scale, 14,000 years or so of First Nation habitation in the Americas may sound like eternity, but on a geological or species time scale, such habitation is very recent contrasted with hominid evolution in Africa.

As Earth hurdles through space, humans use arbitrary and relative parameters to orient themselves such as north-south, up-down, and us-them.

Although global leaders believe economic growth to be the solution to all social problems, that same growth will smack into limits that results, ironically, in economic collapse.

As people mature, they shed older, more limited paradigms and grow into larger ones that explain more about the world.
Station 6 exercise

An evolving participatory stewardship model aims to balance the complexity of nature with that of modern life." —Valle de Oro National Wildlife Refuge
Station 7
Interpretive Framework

From the University to the Field: Socioenvironmental problems cannot be solved from a university campus; they require both virtual and physical extension to communities in order to generate and transfer knowledge, both academic and community-based."
Station 7
CATIE Interpretive Framework

"From the Ancient Road to the Modern Royal Road: The same *Camino Real* (Royal Road) that connected interoceanic and prehispanic commerce became the principal route for the Spanish colonization that extracted gold from the New World and sent it to the Old, thus paving the way for rural and urban settlement in the center of Panama."

"Intersection of Biodiversity: A well-conserved forest is genetically strengthened and strengthens other forests through direct connectivity."

"Safe Distance: Although Western culture impacted the heritage of many indigenous people, the Emberá have conserved their heritage over time, despite being so close to Western culture."

"Water Passage: Chagres National Park does not only contribute 40 percent of the water for the Panama Canal and for the consumption of 1.7 million people, but also contributes to Panama's national image."
Station 7
Chagres National Park Interpretive Framework

"The Salt Route: Commercial traffic along the Salt Route, whether indigenous or Spanish, drove the cultural and territorial domination of El Cocuy and its surroundings."

"Desecration: Despite the fact that the Spanish brought the Holy Cross to extend their religion over the indigenous cosmovision, in reality, they desecrated their land."

"Glacial Masses: Although the snowcap mountains of Güicán, Cocuy, and Chita have one of the most extensive glacial masses north of the equator, the peaks that were once covered in ice, one by one, are melting."

"Biodiversity and Endemism: Given the altitudinal gradient that cuts across extensive forests and paramos and the resulting abundant of habitat, El Cocuy National Park is the heart of high levels of biodiversity and endemism, such as the Frailejón (*Epeletia cleffi*) and collard lizard (*Stenocercus lache*)."

"Commerce along the Salt Route unleashed a wave of desecration of indigenous territory."

"The millennial expansion and retrocession of glaciers in El Cocuy National Park created refuges that permit speciation along altitudinal gradients."
Station 7
El Cocuy National Park Interpretive Framework

"Examining what science has revealed about our evolving universe from the perspective of integral philosophy shows us how evolution is not random, accidental, or otherwise meaningless. On the contrary, its progressive advance reveals the presence of purpose—not an entirely preplanned or externally controlled type of purpose, but rather a creative generation of value that has been continually building upon itself for billions of years." — Steve McIntosh

Station 8
Theme Spotlight: Why Evolution Permeates this Field Guide

Despite the military's requirement that its enlistees behave and dress in uniform manner cannot suppress people's inherent need for self-identity, manifesting, for example, in generations of sailors having turned their iconic Navy crackerjack uniforms into personal canvases.

In Nature, there is an unwritten rule which all creatures respect—except one: you can kill other creatures to meet your needs but never hunt them to extinction. (Based on the Big Idea by author Daniel Quinn)

Though postmodern thinkers have painted the indigenous relationship with nature as harmonious, biodiversity conservationists as well as anthropologists have argued the falsity of this "noble savage" myth, noting deep alterations to natural communities, such as hunting the Pleistocene megafauna into extinction.

As largely terrestrial creatures, humans tend to visualize the surface of the planet as dry land interrupted by water, when in reality, we live on a water world interrupted by islands.

Although we often think of forests as the Earth's lungs, no amount of deforestation has ever altered the 20 percent of the atmosphere that is oxygen; this means that some other force maintains the exact percentage that sustains life, and that secret almost certainly resides in the ocean.

Nature requires all species to move, even the most sedentary—trees, lichen, algal slime—not just to find food but to escape in-breeding and growing too dependent on a single set of environmental conditions.

Early American pioneers looked outward and westward to infinite resources including water and looked inward to a manifest destiny that obliged them to exploit those resources. Now that the West has been won, a new destiny of water use must become manifest before this resource runs dry.

Universal forces combine, coalesce energy, materials, and purpose to create everything unique in the universe, including ourselves.

Because energy is always conserved, no force can dissipate without leaving signs of its passing; therefore, after nearly 15 billion years, scientists still detect the signature of the Big Bang.

Field Notes exercise with students

Interpretive Theme Writer's Worksheet
From the Field Notes of the Interpretive Theme Writer's Field Guide

Date: _____ Organization: _____ Site: _____

Station Two – Primary and Secondary Audiences

Interpreted Object/Topic: _____

Primary Audience (you): _____

Secondary Audience (visitors): _____

Station Three – Kind of Statement

Is the purpose of your Big Idea:

❏ Information ❏ Commercial/marketing

❏ Propaganda ❏ Will/Command/Should

❏ Public Relations ❏ Deception

> Interpretive messages are for the head, from the heart.
> - Steve Van Matre

If you checked any, you are not writing an interpretive theme.

Station Four – Big Idea Inspiration Approaches

Approaches	Write your Big Idea notes
Grammatical	
Big Deal	
Deep Meaning	
Five Whys/So Whats	
Evolutionary Forces	
Irony Revelation	
Freewriting	

Station Four – Big Idea Test

Is your Big Idea...	Yes	No
One complete idea?	❏	❏
Exciting for the primary audience?	❏	❏
Logical, sensical?	❏	❏
Revealing, offering a universal perspective?	❏	❏
Clear, but not necessarily quickly understood?	❏	❏

> Evil hiding among us is an ancient theme.
> - John Carpenter

If you answer "no" to any, rewrite your notes or use another approach.

Station Four – First Draft of Big Idea

_____
_____
_____
_____
_____
_____

> To produce a mighty book, you must choose a mighty theme. No great and enduring volume can ever be written on the flea, though many there be that have tried it. — Herman Melville

Station Five – Provocation Likelihood

Does your Big Idea...	Yes	No
Connect with the audience with known references, examples, and concepts?	☐	☐
Use the audience's language?	☐	☐
Exhibit subject appropriateness?	☐	☐
Apply Knockan Theory (at right)?	☐	☐
Include other spicy ingredients?	☐	☐

If you answer no, reconsider the point.

Higher Interest

Human	Living	Dangerous	Sexual	Surprising	Novel	Extreme Age	Extreme Size
↑	↑	↑	↑	↑	↑	↑	↑
Non-Human	Non-Living	Safe	Non-Sexual	Expected	Ordinary (Normal)	Middle Age	Human Scale

Lower Interest

Items that fall higher on the scale will generate more interest. Indicate where your theme

Station Five – Processing Ease

1. One theme, one idea
2. Readability: keeping sentences and words short
3. Clarity vs. poetry
4. Strong verbs/nouns vs. weak adjectives/adverbs
5. Prohibited words and clichés
6. One powerful figure of speech, example, or anal
7. Word economy vs. wordiness
8. Language and values of audience
9. Active vs. passive voice
10. Power positions

Station Five – Interpretive Theme Draft

_____

_____

_____

Station Five – Strong Theme Test

	Yes	No
Is the theme interpretive rather than some other statement?	☐	☐
Does it provoke rather than just provide easily verifiable information?	☐	☐
Does it avoid postponing the Big Idea?	☐	☐
Does it excite you? Do you want to know more?	☐	☐
Can you imagine an entire program based on it?	☐	☐

When you be with a stro thought provokin theme, you're alre close to success.

– Sam Ha

If you answer "no" to any of these questions, rewrite your theme.

Station Five – Strong Theme for the Secondary Audience

Program Topic: _____

Program Objectives: _____

Audience, goals, values, background: _____

Station Five – Final Theme

_____

_____

_____

_____

To purchase the Interpretive Theme Writer's Field Guide, visit www.pupconsortium.net/theme-writing
For additional ideas on theme writing, see www.facebook.com/heritageinterpretation and www.facebook.com/groups/themethinktank
Worksheet layout by Matt Villamaino

	Suggestions
Round Robin Team Theme Worksheet	
Draft 1 Primary Theme	1. Write a Big Idea in one or two complete sentences related to heritage
	2. New universal perspective, revelatory
	3. Make sure it is an interpretive theme and not some other statement
Evaluator 1 Comments	4. It should excite you
	5. Logical, makes sense
	6. Avoid prohibited words
	7. Apply Knockan Theory
Evaluator 2 Comments	8. Ironies, paradoxes, contrasts
	9. Figures of speech that do not hide meaning
	10. Confront myths
	11. Capture complexity
	12. Brief and economical
	13. Clear, clear
	14. Specific
	15. Active voice
Draft 2 Primary Theme	16. Strong verbs and nouns

Theme Writer: Topic:

Critique of Themes from Real Webinar Participants

The following critique comes from participant contributions during the NAI webinar that inspired this *Field Guide*. Thank you to all those students who participated in that historic moment. Students' comments are in quotes. My suggested comments are bulleted, and my suggested themes are in italics.

Participant 1:

"With needles, thread and gumption, generations of American sailors have turned the iconic Navy crackerjack uniform into their own personal canvases for self expression and style."

- I like the construction of the sentence, the vehicle is clear, has strong, concrete nouns (needs, thread), is specific, and is economically written. Very clear.

- Why is this fact significant? What is the perspective? What does this tell us about sailors, personal expression, navy uniforms? Not sure what the actual focus is. What is the aspect that you would like to provoke in my thoughts?

Despite that the military's requirement that its enlistees behave and dress in uniform manner cannot suppress people's inherent need for self-identity, manifesting, for example, in generations of sailors having turned their iconic Navy crackerjack uniforms into personal canvases.

Attempt 1, participant 2:

"They were used for exhibits developed within the last couple of years. In light of our first session last week, I'm not entirely happy with them now but also not sure how to improve them. Both themes reference refuges located in the Mojave Desert.

"(1) Wildlife, people, and plants depend on Pahranagat's water and diverse landscape. For millennia, these communities flourished on a tradition of respect. If we listen to the land and acknowledge its kinship, we can help restore its natural rhythms for the benefit of all.

"(2) The ancient Corn Creek spring system has attracted wildlife and people for centuries. This rich resource is a dynamic part of the cultural landscape in the Desert National Wildlife Refuge and Las Vegas Valley as a whole. It holds practical and spiritual connections bridged by diverse natural history and cultural significance."

- Contain multiple ideas and purposes

- Imprecise words (#2): "rich resource" (what resource is actually be referred to here?), "dynamic part" (vague language), "as a whole". Which connections and which significance?

- Now survey in search of a nugget or seed of a Big Idea.

- Tradition of respect. What's ecological basis?

In nature, there is an unwritten rule that all creatures respect—except one: you can kill other creatures to meet your needs but never hunt them to extinction. Idea by Daniel Quinn/Ishmael. Somewhat contradicts original intention, so another idea…

Though postmodern thinkers have painted the indigenous relationship with nature as harmonious, biodiversity conservationists as well as anthropologists have argued the falsity of this "noble savage" myth, noting deep alterations to natural communities, such as hunting the Pleistocene megafauna into extinction.

Participant 3
"The ocean is vital to our survival and we share responsibility for protecting it."

- Big Idea vs. Broad Idea

- Way to cover lots of ideas of aquarium is not a Broad Idea

- Interpretive Framework

- Two different statements here

- Too broad for nugget or seed

As largely terrestrial creatures, humans tend to visualize the surface of the planet as dry land interrupted by water, when in reality, we live on a water world interrupted by islands.

Only a change in perspective, let's try something deeper:

Although we often think of forests as the Earth's lungs, no amount of deforestation has ever altered the 20 percent of the atmosphere that is oxygen; this means that some other force maintains the exact percentage that sustains life, and that secret almost certainly resides in the ocean.

Complete certainty isn't necessary for interpretation.

Participant 4
"Context is program delivered onboard a ferry:

"We're not the only travelers here today; birds, whales, and even fish are all going places.

"After day 1 of your workshop, I'm thinking that that theme might benefit from some expansion.

How's this?

"We're not the only travelers here today; birds, whales and even fish are all going places. We share some of the same challenges in getting from place to place—like finding the most efficient way to travel, and making sure we find food."

- Topic: locomotion

- What's the Big Idea about locomotion? What perspective can we reveal that most in your audience does not currently enjoy?

Nature requires all species to move, even the most sedentary—trees, lichen, algal slime—not just to find food but to escape in-breeding and growing too dependent on a single set of environmental conditions.

(Still Participant 4)
"My question is: what I'm working through is the difference (if there is one) between making your theme clear, and giving all the info? Do you think there's room for mystery, as long as it's not so mysterious that your audience doesn't get it?"

I'll give you an example of what I might consider a "mysterious" theme. I'll give the context later, so I don't "spoil" you:

In your quest for the ultimate beachcombers prize, you must follow the signs and be prepared to make sacrifices.

- Not an interpretive theme, does not reveal perspective about interpreted object

- Instructions for a competition

- Clarity for primary audience, could include mystery for second audience but depends. Mystery is variable of Knockan Theory.

- Ham's three strategies for presenting themes

Participant 5

"I work in Papalote Children's Museum. So I developed theme, big idea, and messages about a new exhibit: Del piso al techo, arma tu casa. This is temporary exhibit for children of three to eight years old.

Theme: "The home of my dreams is born in my imagination; I can construct it using sustainable materials."

Big Idea: We can imagine and construct the space of our dreams.

- Two objectives here
- First idea about human creativity, envisioning
- Need assumptions of exhibit to understand the focus for this age group
- Second idea about sustainability. Apt idea for children under seven?
- Research about dreaming of houses?
- Also depends on children's circumstances (homeless?)
- Big Ideas require research and debate

Participant 6

A couple of themes to add to the pot. The first is for a new center that focuses on water and the West.

We need to change our relationship with water. Until now, we have taken it for granted."

What is objective here?

To interpret water in West, need to reveal some perspective or truth about this

What about water in the West do people not understand? Which perspective would allow them to actually do something about the situation which presumably is about decreasing availability?

The use of "we" comes with risk. Some of the audience may take offense since they have not taken water for granted and their relationship may not need improvement and they may not like to be grouped with those for whom this message most applies.

Early American pioneers looked outward and westward to infinite resources including water and looked inward to a manifest destiny that obliged them to exploit those resources. Now that the West has been won, a new destiny of water use must become manifest before this resource runs dry.

"The second is for a swamp stand near to the Everglades that was spared the logger's blade.

"Stories of Fakahatchee speak to richness, adaptability, and endurance."

- Theme has wandered into swamp of vagueness

- It generates too many questions: which stories? What about richness, adaptability, and endurance? What do we think about these topics? What is the conflict in this place? What does it tell us about ecology and the human condition?

- Start over?

Participant 7
"One theme that I have been using for awhile that I am refining starts with a first draft 'Every force on this planet leaves a track.'

"This is refined to a specific audience, let's say a group of new Master Naturalists who are being introduced to an urban nature center, to

"All around us are the tracks of the forces and activities that have shaped our world.

"This leads to the charge "what tracks will you leave."

- Quality theme, economical and has a Big Idea.

- Can it be made stronger? Sure.

- Van Matre has similar idea: Universal forces combine to create unique places.

- Track, better word? Heritage?

- Use Knockan Theory.

Universal forces combine, coalesce energy, materials, and purpose to create everything unique in the universe, including ourselves.

- Knockan Theory factor: Big

Because energy is always conserved, no force can dissipate without leaving signs of its passing; therefore, after nearly 15 billion years, scientists still detect the signature of the Big Bang.

OH MY!

When I worked at the Smithsonian National Museum of Natural History in Washington, D.C., entomologists often displayed their "Oh My!" boxes full of their most prized specimens.

In this *Field Guide*, the Oh My! page contains my favorite themes. You can put yours on the next page.

Sex between people, as well as the spiritual drive to improve the world, are examples of the same creative impulse that has made the universe more complex and mysterious since its beginning: The Big Bang.

The collapse of human civilizations is not a history of slowly degrading ability to provide basic services, but a long ignorance of society's decline by its leaders.

The remote control represents the transformation of the American living room by the couch-centered leisure industry into middle-class society's final resting place.

Behind the artistic beauty of the colonial architecture of Antigua, Guatemala lurks the conquistadors' hidden plan to dominate people's own artistic expression and religious customs.

Many biologists believe that evolution refers only to biology, but in reality, evolution goes much beyond Darwin, beginning with the Big Bang.

Governments fight drug trafficking in Colombia where local farmers grow coca, while invisible and blameless consumers in distant lands drive the demand for cocaine.

What distinguishes World Heritage Sites from other protected areas is the ease with which the Sites can tie together the heart of a person with the heart of humanity.

Raised with unconditional love in Skopje, Mother Theresa demonstrated that while the body must have food, water, air, and shelter to survive, only unconditional love can heal damages to the spirit, open doors closed by hate, and restore even the most indigent to dignity.

Because primary forests bear few if any recognizable signs of humanity, people associate them with prehistory, a time once considered purer and closer to the divine.

Different people with different perspectives interpret the same events through completely different eyes, such as Hurricane Harvey, which could be God's punishment, a random event, or an effect of increasing Climate Chaos.

OH MY!

Write your own…

_____

_____

_____

_____

_____

_____

_____

_____

_____

_____

_____

_____

Recommended and Cited Readings

Berger, Ron, Libby Woodfin, Anne Vilen. 2016. *Learning That Lasts: Challenging, Engaging, and Empowering Students with Deeper Instruction.* Jossey-Bass.

Brochu, Lisa. 2003. *Interpretive Planning.* InterpPress: National Association for Interpretation.

Carvajal, Doreen. 2017. "Let a Robot Be Your Museum Tour Guide." *New York Times.* https://www.nytimes.com/2017/03/14/arts/design/museums-experiment-with-robots-as-guides.html?mcubz=3

Ham, Sam H. 1992. *Environmental Interpretation: A Practical Guide for People with Big Ideas and Small Budgets.* North American Press. Golden, CO.

Ham, Sam H. 2013. *Interpretation: Making a Difference on Purpose.* Fulcrum Publishing: Golden, CO.

Kohl, Jon. 2004. "Mighty Messages Make Memorable Presentations." *Legacy* 15(1): 42–44.

Kohl, Jon. 2014. "Achieving Self-Worth and Self-Identity." Interpretation Journal 19(1): 24–26. http://www.ahi.org.uk/www/resources/subcategory/56/

Leftridge, Alan. 2006. *Interpretive Writing.* InterpPress: National Association for Interpretation.

Lundberg, Ann. 1997. "Toward a thesis-based interpretation." *Legacy* 8(2) 14-16; 30-31.

McIntosh, Steve. 2012. *Evolution's Purpose: An Integral Interpretation of the Scientific Story of Our Origins.* New York: SelectBooks, Inc.

Serrell, Beverly. 2015. *Exhibit Labels: An Interpretive Approach.* Second Edition. Rowman & Littlefield. New York.

Stanfield, Brian R. 2002. *The Workshop Book: From Individual Creativity to Group Action.* Gabriola Island, British Columbia: New Society Publishers.

Swimme, Brian & Mary Evelyn Tucker. 2014. *Journey of the Universe.* New Haven: Yale University Press.

Van Matre, Steve. 2008. *Interpretive Design and the Dance of Experience.* Institute for Earth Education.

Wells, Marcela, Barbara H. Butler, & Judith Koke. 2013. *Interpretive Planning for Museums: Integrating Visitor Perspective in Decision Making.* Routledge.

www.speedlevitch.com
Website of a famous and eccentric New York City bus guide (but not interpretive)

Also please visit the Interpretive Theme Writing Think Tank on Facebook moderated by Clark Hancock for continue discussion on this topic.

PUP Global Heritage Consortium

The PUP Consortium is a non-profit global network with the mission to transform the global paradigm in heritage management and planning to a more holistic approach. Its membership specializes in visitor management and heritage interpretation in particular. It promotes the professionalization of interpretation in developing countries especially Latin America where, for instance, it offers a Spanish language interpretation webinar series in collaboration with the National Association for Interpretation. In promoting the transformation, PUP publishes, offers courses, and participates in other learning activities. It has co-sponsored not only this book but a book on holistic planning very useful for interpretive planning called *The Future Has Other Plans: Planning Holistically to Conserve Natural and Cultural Heritage* by Jon Kohl and PUP board member Steve McCool. This book was edited by Sam Ham in his Applied Communication Series published by Fulcrum, the same press that published Sam's interpretation books. PUP also co-sponsored the publication *Esencia de la Interpretación Ambiental: Visión holística para experimentar y conservar el patrimonio natural y cultural de América Latina*, by Marisol Mayorga and Jon Kohl. It is the first university textbook on heritage interpretation written for the Latin American audience, published by Editorial UNED in Costa Rica. In October 2018, PUP coorganized the First Latin American Congress on Heritage Interpretation with the support of NAI.

Global Heritage Consortium

WEBINARIOS SOBRE
INTERPRETACIÓN
DEL PATRIMONIO

CONGRESO LATINOAMERICANO
DE INTERPRETACIÓN
DEL PATRIMONIO

MÉXICO COSTA RICA COLOMBIA
PERÚ GUATEMALA

Theme Writing:
A Trail That Never Ends

Tree swallows. Jewelweed. Decaying log. Turtles. Yellow-lady slipper orchid. Woodpecker hole. Poison Ivy. What do these things have in common? Virtually nothing. Nothing, except they were all signs along a self-guided nature trail. I remember these signs because many years ago I helped maintain the trail and signs. In fact, I am probably the only person alive who remembers these signs. In those days, generic nature trails with miscellaneous interpretive signs about things along the trail were commonplace. Now due to the efforts of Dr. Sam Ham and others, including the author of this *Field Guide*, we learned that a thematic approach to interpretation is more effective to achieving understanding and retention of strategic messages, rather than merely presenting random facts about whatever objects that happen to be present. Thankfully, trails like the one described above are becoming rarer as interpretive planners establish thematic trails. Likewise, programs and exhibits have benefited from thematic approaches.

Interpretive Theme Writer's Field Guide advances this understanding to new audiences and gives practical applications of thematic interpretation along its own trail marked by the stations. Like field guides to flowers or birds, this book describes thematic interpretation so that the reader will be able to identify it when they see it. This *Field Guide* distinguishes themes from information dissemination and other communications. It illustrates the differences between strong themes and

An acorn woodpecker jumps from a hole in a tree.

weak themes. It then gives detailed instruction on how to write powerful themes and how to communicate them to specific audiences.

The practical advice shared in preceding pages will enhance the effectiveness of interpreters regardless of the medium they are using to communicate their messages. *Interpretive Theme Writer's Field Guide* takes thematic interpretation approaches into the field, promotes their use, and makes application of thematic interpretation straightforward.

Readers of this short, but important, book will not look at interpretive programs or trails in the same way again. And they certainly would not allow an interpretive trail like the one I maintained many years ago.

Now go into the world with this *Field Guide* in hand and craft great themes!

Dr. Ted Cable
Retired Professor of Heritage Interpretation
Department of Park Management and Conservation
Kansas State University

A
academic publishing, 19
active voice, 81
adjectives, 68, 79
Allende, Isabel, 45, 75
alliteration, 72
Angelou, Maya, 46
approaches to inspiration, 49–57
argument presentation, 41, 84
Aristotle, 46
Armstrong, Neil, 47
artifacts, 47
artificial intelligence, 111–112
audience
    big idea suggestions, 31
    disagreement, 63
    exercise, 32
    knowledge of, 19, 27–28
    primary, 28–29, 31–32
    relevance of provocative themes, 67–68
    secondary, 29, 32
    spotlight, 33
    vehicle to mobilize, 67–68

B
Bateson, Gregory, 63
Beck, Larry, 41
Berger, Ron, 36
Bergson, Henri, 77
big deal approach, 49–51
big ideas
    interpretive theme vs., 37–38
    qualities of, 47, 57–60
    term usage, 35–36
    test, 64
    vehicle for, 36–38, 67–68
Blake, William, 80
Bohm, David, 97
Bokova, Irina, 96
Bowen, Elizabeth, 71
Brahms, Johannes, 48
brevity, 75–76
Brochu, Lisa, 30, 61
Burr, Ty, 79

C
Cable, Ted, 41
CATIE Theme, 101
Chaco Culture National Historic Park, New Mexico, 50
Chagres National Park, Panama, 42, 88, 107, 132
civilizations, 47, 50
clarity, 59–60, 80
clichés, 79–80
Cohen, Andrew, 37
commercial/marketing statements, 22
committees, 88
community development
    meanings and heritage, 95–97
    theme writing, 87
complexity, 72
concepts, 46–47
conclusions, 100
contemplation-mediation approach, 55–57
creative teams, 87

D
data, correlation or causation, 47
deception, 22
deep meaning approach, 51
Deming, W. Edward, 59
DesCartes, René, 71
direction to presentations, 27
distance influences, 72
documentation, 89

E
Edison, Thomas, 49
education, 19
Einstein, Albert, 46, 72
El Cocuy National Park, Colombia, 71, 108
Elbow, Peter, 54
emergent model, 28
emerging themes, 88, 100, 106
Emerson, Ralph Waldo, 59, 80
empty-calorie words, 79
Environmental Interpretation (Ham), 30, 36, 49, 75

evidence, supporting, 60
evolutionary forces approach, 52–53
Evolution's Purpose (McIntosh), 113
exhibit labels, 20, 21
experience, 48

F
facts, presentation of, 58
factual statement (theme), 41
feedback loops, 55, 89
figurative language, 76–77
fill-in-the-blank theme, 61–63
five whys/so what (Socratic) approach, 52
Flint Hills Discovery Center, Kansas, 72, 96, 99
Floyd, William, 62
Forrester, Jay, 55
Fort Jesus National Monument, Kenya, 61, 71, 81
Freeman, Martin, 29
freewriting approach, 54–55
Frost, Robert, 78
Fuller, Buckminster, 59, 79

G
generality, specificity vs., 81
Goldberg, 54
grammatical approach, 49

H
Ham, Sam
    argument for interpretation, 41
    Environmental Interpretation (Ham), 30, 36, 49, 75
    one-sentence rule for themes, 75
    theme writing vs. theme development, 39
    thought-provoking themes, 69
Hawking, Stephen, 58
heritage, 46, 95–97
higher-level themes, 108
historical scans, 102
humanity, added to non-humans, 74

I
ideas, identifying, 40
    See also big ideas
Illinois River Valley, Chicago, 103, 104
imagery, 77
implicit model, 28

influences, over time and distance, 72
information/subject statements, 22
inspiration
    approaches, 49–57
    big idea qualities, 57–60
    big idea suggestions, 46–47, 63
    big ideas test, 64
    meaning-making process, 45–46
    topic, 47–49
    universal relevance, 61–63
Institute for Cultural Affairs, 96
interpretive framework
    big idea suggestions, 103
    exercise, 107–108
    format, 103
    meanings and heritage, 95–97
    reasons for using, 97
    steps to facilitate, 98–101
interpretive intelligence, 111–113
interpretive theme, big ideas vs., 37–38
interpretive Theme Writer's Worksheet, 145–147
interpretive themes
    argument presentation, 41
    big idea suggestions, 35–38
    exercise, 40
    objective and big idea, 42
    theme writing vs. theme development, 39
    vehicle to mobilize, 36–38
    visual aids and objects, 39
irony, 71, 77
irony revelation approach, 53–54

J
Jefferson, Thomas, 46, 88
Journey of the Universe (documentary), 113

K
Kerckhove, Derrick de, 69, 137
Kim, Daniel, 59
Knockan Theory, 69, 137–138
Kuhn, Thomas, 71

L
Learning that Lasts (Berger, Woodfin, and Vilen), 47, 134
letter to offer support for interpreters, 90, 91
Lincoln, Abraham, 46

logic, in presentations, 58
Lundberg, Ann, 41, 58, 59

M
Machiavelli, Niccolò, 71
material, behavior of, 47
McCullers, Carson, 80
McIntosh, Steve, 113
Meadows, Donella, 52
meaning, 45–46, 95–97, 103
message, theme vs., 25
metaphor, 76, 80
methodology, theme writing, 88
metonymy, 77
Miller, Ron, 75
More, Thomas, 76
Mother Teresa House, Skopje, Macedonia, 73
mystery, 68, 69
myths, 72

N
nouns, 80

O
Oberst, Conor, 79
objective, big idea and, 42
objectives
    of Field Guide, 16
    related to interpretation, 23
Oh My! boxes, 154–158
Oliver, Mary, 81
one-sentence rule for themes, 75, 76
orientation, 19
Orr, David, 78
Ortberg, John, 82

P
Panshin, Alexei, 67
paradox, 71
passive voice, 81
Perkins, David, 36
personal relationships, 19
personification, 77
persons, 46
perspectives, 50, 53, 58
physical geography, 47
Picasso, Pablo, 79
poetry, 78, 80
power positions, 82

preparation step, 100
primary audience, 28–29, 31–32, 58
primary theme, 29–31
proceedings, 100
professional consultant writers, 89
propaganda, 19, 22
provocation, 58–59
provocative themes
    process of, 75–82
    relevance of, 67–72, 75
public relations, 19, 22
PUP Consortium, 95, 98
pushback, 63

R
readability, 75–77
reading widely, 48
relevance of provocative themes, 67–68
repetition, 72
revelation-irony theme, 56
revelatory perspectives, 58
rhythm, 72
Rice, Anne, 35
Rite of Passage (Panshin), 67
The Road Not Taken (Orr), 78
robots, 111–112
Rosero, Carlos, 89

S
sandwich model, 28
scale, theme writing, 87
secondary audience, 29, 32
secondary themes, 33
Senge, Peter, 36
Serrell, Beverly, 20, 21, 35, 48–49
Smith, John, 62
social marketing, 25
Socratic approach, 52
specificity, 81
statements, types of, 22
statements of will, 19
strong theme examples, 131–144
strong theme test, 82
strong themes, 24, 35–42, 61, 83
subject appropriateness, 72
subjective adjectives, 79
sub-themes, 31, 33
suspense, 69
Swimme, Brian, 76
synecdoche, 77

T

The Talmud, 46
Tayrona National Park, Columbia, 102, 103
team work
  importance of, 16, 87–88
  theme teams, 89–91
TED.com talk, 46
tension, 71
Thematic, Organized, Relevant, and
  Entertaining (TORE), 20
thematic interpretation
  big idea suggestions, 21
  context, 20–21
  exercises, 22–23
  forms of, 19
  heritage management connection, 20
  spotlight, 24–25
theme descriptions, 101
theme selection, 30, 31
theme writing
  big idea suggestions, 92
  exercise, 92
  letter to offer support for interpreters, 90,
    91
  levels, 87–89
  professional writer's role, 89
theme writing vs. theme development, 39
themes
  critique of, from webinar participants,
    148–153
  emerging, 88, 100, 106
  higher-level, 108
  message vs. theme, 25
  primary, 29–31
  theme of themes, 17
  universal relevance, 61–62
  weak vs. strong, 24
time influences, 72
Tocqueville, Alexis de, 75
Toffler, Alvin, 25
topics, 30, 31, 47–49
transformative themes, 73
truths, 61–63

U

UNESCO, 96
universal forces, 52
universal processes, 100
universal relevance, 61–63
Utopia (More), 76

V

vagueness, 81
Valle de Oro National Wildlife Refuge,
  Albuquerque, New Mexico, 30, 72, 83,
  96, 98, 99, 101
Van Matre, Steve, 52, 96, 152
vehicle to mobilize big ideas, 36–38, 67–68
verbs, for stronger themes, 53, 80, 125–130
Vilen, Anne, 36
vision, 36
visual aids and objects, 39
voice, active vs. passive, 81

W

weak themes, 24, 83
wide-ranging reading, 48
Wilber, Ken, 73
will/command/should statements, 22
Wise, Robert, 47
Woodfin, Libby, 36
Woodhouse, Mark, 59
word economy, 75–76
wording techniques, 72, 76–77
words, suggestions and cautions
  adjectives, 68, 79
  clichés, 79–80
  empty-calorie words, 79
  irony, 53
  verbs for stronger themes, 53, 125–130
  you/we/us, 77, 79
worksheet, for theme writers, 145–147
Workshop Method of the Technology of
  Participation, 96, 98
World Heritage City, Antigua, Guatemala,
  56

Z

Zimbardo, Philip, 77